JERK FROM JAMAICA

JERK FROM JAMAICA

BARBECUE CARIBBEAN STYLE

HELEN WILLINSKY

PHOTOGRAPHS BY

ED ANDERSON

Ten Speed Press

10

Ten Speed Press
PO Box 7123
Berkeley, California 94707
www.tenspeed.com
Distributed in Australia by Simon and Schuster Australia,
in Canada by Ten Speed Press Canada, in New Zealand by
Southern Publishers Group, in South Africa by Real Books, and
in the United Kingdom and Europe by Publishers Group UK.

Cover and text design by Ed Anderson
Library of Congress Cataloging-in-Publication Data
Willinsky, Helen.
  Jerk from Jamaica : barbecue Caribbean style /
Helen Willinsky ; photography by Ed Anderson. -- Rev. ed.
    p. cm.
  Rev. ed. of : Jerk: Barbecue from Jamaica.
  Freedom, Calif. : Crossing Press, 1990.
  Includes index.
  ISBN-13: 978-1-58008-842-8 (pbk.)
  ISBN-10: 1-58008-842-2 (pbk.)
  1. Cookery, Jamaican. 2. Barbecue cookery.
  I. Willinsky, Helen. Jerk: Barbecue from Jamaica. II. Title.
  TX716.J27W55 2007
  641.597292--dc22
                    2006037605
Printed in China
First printing, 2007
1 2 3 4 5 6 7 8 9 10 — 11 10 09 08 07

ACKNOWLEDGMENTS

I would like to take a little space to acknowledge and thank some dear friends and colleagues who have been instrumental in helping to make jerk the national obsession it has become, and who shared some of their recipes with me for this new edition of *Jerk from Jamaica*.

Winston Stona, whose line of Busha Browne products has brought jerk flavors to barbecue lovers around the world, contributed recipes for Jamaican Jerk Pork (page 31); Jerk Sweet Potato Oven Fries (page 117); Avocado and Papaya Gazpacho (page 123);

Norma Shirley has taken Jamaican cuisine to a whole new level from her base, Norma's on the Terrace at the Devon House. For this new edition, she graciously gave me recipes for Jerk Baked Black Beans (page 122); Sautéed Mushrooms à la Jerk (page 122); Jamaican Jerk Meatballs (page 102); and Passion Fruit Martini (page 161);

Virginia Burke of Walkerswood, which started as a rural community cottage industry to create employment for its people, has taken jerk seasoning and helped move it into every nook and cranny in the countryside. For this new edition, she gave me Stuffed Jerk Pork Roll with Plantains (page 30) and Jerk Shrimp Salad (page 81).

Dennis Hayes has been a champion of this book from the very beginning; for this edition he also contributed his barbecue expertise and some wonderful recipes: Jerk Chicken "Hash" (page 49); Jammin' Roast Potatoes (page 118); and Blue Lagoon (page 161).

PUBLISHER'S NOTE

Some of the recipes in this book include raw eggs, meat, or fish. When these foods are consumed raw, there is always the risk that bacteria, which is killed by proper cooking, may be present. For this reason, when serving these foods raw, always buy certified salmonella-free eggs and the freshest meat and fish available from a reliable grocer, storing them in the refrigerator until they are served. Because of the health risks associated with the consumption of bacteria that can be present in raw eggs, meat, and fish, these foods should not be consumed by infants, small children, pregnant women, the elderly, or any persons who may be immunocompromised.

To my parents,
George and Marion

CONTENTS

The secrets of jerk cooking were well kept for many years. Not until about thirty years ago did this delectable flavor indulgence reach the mainstream Jamaican table. Helen Willinsky was certainly part of this liberation, with her "Helen's Jerk" products. Before the advent of commercially bottled seasoning, jerk pork or jerk-anything-else was basically street food and seldom made at home. Now jerk is enjoyed worldwide.

In this wonderful book Helen brings to light the essence of jerk cooking. Her accounts of authentic Jamaican life spill forth with adept storytelling ease as she takes the reader through jerk's culinary history and her personal cooking experiences.

Jamaican food has the unfortunate reputation of being hot and *only* hot. Traditional jerk did nothing to dispel this notion, because a fiery jerk really is a thrill for those who love very spicy food. Helen, like most Jamaicans, knows the difference between hot and spicy, and teaches that you can turn up or lower the heat to your own desire. She builds basic recipes for making traditional jerk, then expertly deconstructs and reworks her recipes into an array of modern and innovative versions. The recipes in *Jerk from Jamaica* take you through the various spices and foodstuffs used in our cooking. You'll learn to use ingredients like ginger, tamarind, and coconut in savory dishes and flip out your taste buds without singeing them.

Like every cuisine, jerk is constantly evolving: great cooks are creative by nature and are influenced by new trends and popular cooking styles. "Jerk" used to refer only to a pig grilled slowly over a fire-pit of pimento wood. Nowadays when you say "jerk," most people will assume the main ingredient could be chicken, pork, and maybe more. Helen's recipes use a wide variety of meats and seafood, and they also allow for ingredient substitutions, all the while making sure you understand the roots and traditions of jerk cooking. Here you'll find everything from meatballs to fajitas, from lobster to scallops to salmon.

Helen's recipes also offer several cooking styles to choose from: she walks you through all the details of preparing barbecue, stovetop, or oven versions of jerk recipes, including dealing with gas fire, wood chips, and coals in a barbecue grill. Her selection of recipes takes into account her readers' need to prepare all kinds of dishes, from a simple salad for two to more complex dishes for entertaining. There is a wonderful array of side dishes, like rice and peas and baked or fried plantains, which root the meals in Jamaican tradition, and a choice of fruity dipping sauces and chutney to accompany main dishes. Desserts include wonderful Jamaican flavors like coffee, lime, and rum, and there are drinks and cocktails to make your head spin. How about a "Bloody Mary à la Jerk" for starters!

I think her recipe choices are heartwarming and family-friendly at the core. No doubt everyone with a copy of this book will find brand new enthusiasm for firing up the coals and doing a Jamaican 'ting.

Virginia Burke
Director of Marketing, Walkerswood Caribbean Foods
Author of *Eat Caribbean* and *Walkerswood Caribbean Kitchen*
December 2006

WHAT IS JERK?

Jerk cooking is an authentic Jamaican method of cooking pork, chicken, seafood, beef, fruits, and vegetables over a fire pit or on a barbecue grill. But it is the highly spiced special seasoning—a combination of scallions, onions, thyme, pimento (Jamaican allspice), cinnamon, nutmeg, chilies, and salt—that makes jerk what it is. To me, jerk cooking is the perfect reflection of the Jamaican lifestyle: spicy, sweet, and hot.

Jerk seasonings are hot with chilies, but, as you savor jerked food, the variety of spices catches up with you, and it is like a carnival where all the elements come together in your mouth. The combination of spices tastes as if they were quarreling and dancing and mingling in your mouth all at the same time. It is not a predictable flavor, but rather a hot, spicy, uncontrolled festival that engages all your senses. It is so unexpected a taste that, in spite of its peppery heat, you automatically want more. We have a saying in Jamaica, "It is very morish."

People always ask me, "How did jerk get its name?" I really don't know, but I can tell you that almost everyone has a pet theory. "Jerk" may be related to *charqui,* an Incan word that means, basically, jerky or dried meat—some speculate that Spanish sailors who landed in both Peru and Jamaica made the connection. Some people say it is called jerk because the meat is turned over and over again—or jerked over and over again—as it cooks over the fire. Others say that is not right; it is called jerk because, when it is served, the jerk man pulls—or jerks—a portion of meat off the pork. To me, it does not matter what it is called, or why. What counts is flavor.

The spices that are used in jerk seasoning have a special pungency. Jamaican spices are world famous—their oil content is said to be higher than that of any other spices in the world, and it is this oiliness that intensifies the zip and zest. (It is even said that in World War I, European soldiers were told to line their boots with pimento to keep their feet warmer in the cold winters.)

Jerk huts are everywhere in Jamaica. You see them clustered by the side of the road, a medley of structures. There is always a wonderful smoky aroma hovering over the huts: the pungency of burning pimento wood and spices mingling with the delicious scent of the meat. And everywhere are buses, trucks, cars, and vans disgorging hungry passengers in search of jerk pork, jerk chicken, escovitch fish, salt fish, ackee, roast yams, roast plantains, boiled corn, rice and peas, cock soup, mannish water, Irish moss, and festival! You can hear the cries from each hut: "Which jerk you want?" "Taste mine!" Everything Jamaicans love is found at the jerk huts, embellished with a great deal of spice.

Jerk huts are usually octagonal or circular, built around a telephone pole that supports the thatched or shingled roof. There is a seating bar around the outside of the hut. The food is jerked outside, either in a lean-to attached to the hut, or in a separate hut of its own, or even under a tree. There is rarely any such thing as a parking lot—you park on the side of the road, and you are greeted warmly by the proprietor and amiable strangers there as you join the other customers, who are impatiently waiting to sink their teeth into the delicious slabs of meat.

All jerk huts and shacks are very casual affairs, but if it is an especially rustic jerk hut, you can saunter over and pick out what you want directly from the fire. The jerk man or lady will then use a cleaver to slice off whatever you have requested and will probably weigh it to know how much to charge you. The meat is served wrapped in aluminum foil or placed on a paper plate. Pork is usually cubed for you on the spot, and you can stand right there

and eat it with your fingers. Chicken tends to be a bit juicier than pork, so you really need several napkins to handle that. Usually the meat is very tender because it has been marinated for some time and then cooked slowly. In addition to pork and chicken, you can usually buy jerk sausage, and even jerked lobster if you are on the northern coast of the island.

You must always eat jerk with something sweet or bland to cut the heat—either some festival, which is a little like a sweet hush puppy, or some hard dough bread, which is a soft, flat, bagel-style bread. Of course, you must cool your mouth with Jamaican Red Stripe beer, Ting grapefruit soda, or a rum concoction. And there is usually music, music, music.

In Jamaica, the best place to look for jerk is in Boston, near Boston Beach, the home of the original jerk pits. The Pork Pit in Montego Bay and the Ocho Rios Jerk Center are also famous jerk pits. In Negril, jerk pits line the two main roads that lead in and out of town; in Port Antonio, look for jerk in West Street, near the market.

Pork has been jerked in Jamaica at least since the mid-seventeenth century. Methods of pit cooking were brought to the island by African slaves, and these methods were probably the beginnings of jerk cooking techniques—though the native West Indians also cooked food on green wood lattices over open fires. Quite possibly the enslaved West African hunters adapted the seasoning methods of the native Arawak Indians, especially in their use of chilies. But it was not until the mid-eighteenth century, during the guerrilla wars between the escaped ex-slaves, known as

Maroons, and the English, that there was any real record of jerk seasoning being used to prepare pork.

To the Maroon guerrilla bands, the little wild boars that darted through the brush were a wonderful source of food. While some men kept watch on the movements of the redcoats on the plains, others, equipped with long spears, undertook the equally arduous task of pursuing the slippery animals to their lairs in the almost inaccessible parts of the mountains.

Caught and killed at last, the boars were brought down from the mountaintops on long sticks to provide food for the weary rebels. Although some meat was eaten at the time of the hunt, most had to be preserved until the next opportunity to hunt presented itself—and who could tell when that would be?

Jerk seasoning, which is laced heavily with salt and peppers, kept the meat from spoiling. The pork was slathered with the aromatic spice combination and wrapped in leaves. When it came time to cook the meat, the wrapped marinated pig would be put in a hole in the ground filled with hot stones to steam slowly in its own juices. Or, it would be grilled slowly—for 12 or 14 hours—over a fire of green wood, which burns slowly and smokes a lot. By the time a peace treaty was finally signed by the opposing forces, jerking pork was deep in the Jamaican psyche.

Nowadays, it is common to barbecue pork over pimento wood, which gives the meat a unique, tangy flavor, but the early Maroons used the wood of other trees, plus a number of strange herbs. The practice was always a secret and, even today, if you ask the descendant of a Maroon where his wood and herbs can be found, he will wave his hand vaguely toward the surrounding hills, and say, "Over there."

Jerking meat has become much more widely known by non-Jamaicans over the last few decades. Tourists began discovering jerk by visiting the huts on the north shore of the island, and as tourism grew, the number of jerk huts grew. Now there are jerk huts everywhere—in every town, every village, every city in Jamaica.

Jerking is no longer confined to pork but now includes fish and chicken. Although jerk pork originally led the field, jerk chicken is now most popular. In Kingston, the capital of Jamaica, the demand for jerk chicken on weekends is incredible. Steel drums converted to grills are now ubiquitous. They line the streets and, on a weekend in certain areas, so much smoke emerges from the line of drums that, except for the smell, you might imagine that a San Francisco fog had come to Jamaica.

Jerk is a savory, flavorful result of the combination of African and native cultures on the island. Jamaicans are great harmonizers—we make delicious soups, we keep our friends forever, we are fantastic musicians and artists—and we have applied this same harmony to our jerk seasoning.

All Jamaicans have their own variations on jerk. "Come and taste my jerk chicken," we hear again and again. "It is better than the last time I saw you." Some make liquid marinades, others make thick pastes or spice rubs to massage into the meats. Many of these concoctions are made at home. So you don't have to go to a Jamaican jerk hut to enjoy jerk. You can make it in your own kitchen, just as the Jamaicans do.

CHAPTER 1

JERKING BASICS
AND JERK SEASONINGS

This chapter includes recipes and techniques for seasoning and making authentic jerk in your own backyard barbecue grill, oven, or stove-top smoker. You don't have to dig a pit in your yard to make great Jamaica jerk barbecue. Let me tell you how we do it in the islands and then I will give you methods for creating jerk barbecue on your home grill or smoker.

If you can't come to Jamaica to visit a jerk pit and view how we cook, I will now tell you how we barbecue Jamaica style. First, the meat, usually a pork shoulder, is slathered with seasonings and left to marinate for at least three or four hours. Then, while the meat is marinating, a pit is dug and lined with rocks, and a fire is made in it using mainly the wood of the pimento (allspice) tree. When the fire has died down to burning embers, the meat is wrapped in foil (although in the past the meat would have been wrapped in tree leaves) then placed in the fire and covered with the burning coals. The pit is covered with tree branches or some other cover, often a piece of zinc sheet metal, with

the fire carefully maintained by the pit master, who stokes the fire occasionally with more wood. The meat then cooks with a combination of low heat and smoke for four to six hours, until it's tender. The meat is taken from the pit and then either pulled apart with forks, in a motion that would resemble "jerking," or chopped into portion pieces with a cleaver.

At the jerk huts, which have mushroomed throughout the entire island, you will find all the different jerk dishes, from larger and more dense cuts of meat such as pork, which require low heat with smoke and slow cooking in the pit method, to chicken and fish, which are better suited to cooking with more heat over a grill. Marinated chicken or whole fish will cook for 30 to 40 minutes over a medium fire on a grill. Some pork roasts are flattened or, as your butcher may call it, "butterflied," to spread out the surface of the meat for quicker cooking, then covered with spices and cooked over a grill at low temperatures for about two to three hours.

Jerk Cooking

Some vendors use old oil drums for jerking. They cover the drum with pieces of zinc roofing to trap the juices and smoke, which makes the chicken or pork tender. At the end of the cooking time, the cover is removed and the meat grills to a crisp finish. This is my favorite method, because the meat is tender on the inside and crisp on the outside.

You can create a similar effect in your home by roasting larger cuts of meat or a whole chicken in a very slow oven (225° to 250°F) for 2 to 3 hours, then finishing the cooking by grilling the meat over charcoal.

BARBECUE GRILLS

In Jamaica, fifty-gallon steel drums are converted into grills. Chicken prepared on them is known as "pan chicken," which comes from the name given to the steel drums that are converted into musical instruments, also known as "pans." The same flavor can be achieved on a backyard barbecue grill. Use charcoal briquets, hardwood charcoal, wood, or propane, or a combination of these fuels, with the food on a grill placed about six inches above the fire, and then you can adjust the heat level to match the cooking time needed for the food you are cooking.

If using charcoal, don't fill the grill with more charcoal than you need; it takes longer to light and burn down, but you can continue to add more pieces of charcoal to maintain your desired heat level. Spread out one layer of charcoal just to the dimensions of the foods that will be cooked, then mound the charcoal to light it. You can also use hardwood charcoal, which takes a little more effort to light, but the resulting flavor is well worth the effort. Use a "chimney": stack the hardwood charcoal with some paper in the bottom of the chimney and then light it. About 30 minutes after you have lit the fire, spread out the coals again. For smoking or slow cooking, place a drip pan in the back of the grill and make an indirect fire by arranging the coals in front of the drip pan. The food will go directly over the drip pan. (This is also a good way to prevent flare-ups when cooking high-fat foods.) You can use a disposable aluminum pan, or make a shallow bowl using aluminum foil. The juices that drip into the pan can be collected and poured over the meat for additional flavor and moistness. You will need to monitor your heat regularly, checking your fire perhaps every 20 or 30 minutes to determine if you need to add a bit more fuel. If you do need to, add more fuel sparingly, as you don't want to stoke the heat too quickly. It is easier to bring the heat up slowly with a few pieces of fuel than to cool down a hot fire.

If you have a gas grill with two or more burners with controls for each burner, turn on one burner to low heat to cook, and place the drip pan on the burner that is off with the food cooking above it on the grill. Adding wood chips to your fire will provide additional flavor (Jamaican pimento wood is ideal if you can purchase some, otherwise woods such as apple, hickory, or oak will do just fine). Soak a generous handful of chips in water for about 30 minutes so they won't burn up immediately. Drain them, then sprinkle them over the coals any time during cooking and cover the grill, if possible, for 5 to 10 minutes so that the smoke permeates the meat (if your grill does not have a lid, you can fashion a loose tent of aluminum foil over the food instead). If you are using a gas grill, I have a clever little trick taught to me by a pit master. Take a handful of the wood chips that have been soaking in water and shake off some of the water. Place the chips on a small sheet of aluminum foil and then fold the foil to make a pouch. Puncture the foil four or five times in the top and bottom, then place the pouch on top of a gas burner. The heat from the burner will slowly burn the wood chips and allow the smoke to slowly slip through the holes to flavor your meat. There are also premade wood chip pans that you can buy at your favorite shop for barbecue gadgets and tools.

CONTROLLING THE HEAT OF A BARBECUE GRILL

I think larger cuts of meat are most delicious when cooked slowly over a low fire. A very hot fire will char the meat on the outside and leave it raw on the inside, which may be desired for steaks and chops, but thick cuts of brisket and pork need tender cooking, low and slow!

You can control the heat of your fire by making sure to let the fire burn down to coals before you start cooking, and by spreading the coals out evenly and adjusting the distance of the grill grate from the fire. If your grill has an adjustable vent, you can open or close it to adjust the amount of air getting to the fire: closed will make the fire burn more slowly, open will increase oxygen and raise the heat. My Aunt Becky taught me that when the fire is just the right temperature for grilling quickly you can hold your hand about one inch above the grill grate for three seconds (with your hand over the grill, say the words "one Jamaica, two Jamaica, three Jamaica!") before you have to take your hand away. A low fire, which is required for larger pieces of meat and whole chickens, will allow you to hold your hand over the grill grate for six to eight seconds. You can easily purchase a thermometer for your grill these days, and many grills and smokers have them already installed, making it much easier to control your heat. Low heat will mean a range of 225° to 250°F, medium heat 300° to 350°F, and high heat 400°F.

Sometimes, when the oil from the marinade or the fat from the meat drips onto the hot coals, a flame will flare up and char the meat. You can control flare-ups by sprinkling the coals with water from a spray bottle kept handy for that purpose. A drip pan to catch the fat as it drips will also prevent flare-ups.

OPEN-PIT COOKING

If you really want to re-create the true Jamaican jerk, you must get out your shovel and go to work. Dig a pit about two feet deep, four feet long, and three feet wide. A few hours before you are ready to eat, build a wood fire in the pit. In Jamaica we use pimento (Jamaican allspice) wood, or a combination of pimento wood and charcoal, but you can use any type of hardwood, with the wood filling half the pit about two-thirds of the way to the top. Wait until the wood has burned down

3

to coals and you have a medium (about 350°F), smoky fire before you begin to cook. From time to time, you will need to add more wood to the fire, but keep the fresh-burning wood away from the cooking meat—the heat should be indirect.

Place the grill grate over the pit and put the marinated meat on it. A pork roast will take about two hours to cook, a whole chicken will take about an hour, and a whole fish will cook in 20 to 30 minutes, depending on its size. As the meat cooks, turn it frequently and continue to add small amounts of wood from time to time to keep your heat level even.

This type of pit cooking is the authentic method used in the "old days," but nowadays many of the jerk pits have come to look like unusual contraptions of metal and wood that resemble crude grills. Your results will not really be different if you use a pit, but you will enjoy the rustic appeal of this cooking method.

STOVE-TOP SMOKERS

Not everyone can live in a place like Jamaica, where the weather is suitable for outdoor grilling year-round. Those people might want to acquire a stove-top smoker, which can give meat seasoned with jerk spices that desired open-pit or barbecue grill flavor even when cooked indoors.

A stove-top smoker, or water pan smoker, consists of a stack of pans. The bottom pan holds soaked wood chips. Above that is a pan that holds water, vinegar, wine, or fruit juice—whatever you want to use to flavor your meat. In the top pan is a grate on which you place the meat. The water (or other cooking liquid) combined with the wood chips makes an aromatic smoke that infuses the meat with great flavor. To use, follow the manufacturer's directions. Generally, it takes about 20 minutes to cook four chicken breasts in a stove-top smoker, and 5 to 10 minutes to cook a batch of shrimp. Meat cooked in a water smoker will be moist and tender, but bear in mind that the stove-top smokers have a limited capacity, so they are intended for cuts of meat such as chicken breasts, steaks, chops, and tenderloins that can fit in the cooker. I like to finish the meat on a grill or under a broiler to get a crisp exterior; this is not necessary but it does add a wonderful texture to your meat.

OUTDOOR SMOKERS

There are several styles of smokers available that yield wonderful results when cooking jerk barbecue. These smokers differ from grills in that they will have the fire chamber further away from the grill and allow space for placing a water pan near the fire. Instructions for proper smoking will vary by make and manufacturer, so the best recommendation is to follow the instructions given in the manual.

How to Tell When Your Jerk Is Done

When cooking any meat, the most difficult thing to gauge is when the food is done. Suggested cooking times can be given in recipes, but whether the meat is at room temperature or refrigerator-cold when placed on the grill, how thick the meat or fish is, how hot the fire is, and how far from the fire the grill grate is placed—even the weather—will all affect the actual cooking time. Thicker cuts of meat will cook more evenly if the meat is allowed to come to room temperature before placing it on the grill, but use caution and do not leave the meat out any longer than it needs to get to room temperature; this is especially true with poultry.

Experienced cooks can tell just how done meat is by feel. Well-done meat will feel as firm as the flesh on the palm of your hand. Fish should be opaque throughout and firm to the touch. Juices from poultry should run clear, not red, when the flesh is pricked with a fork. Only experience will enable you to judge when it's time to remove meat, chicken, and fish from a grill.

An instant-read thermometer (available at most kitchen supply stores) is a big help in determining when roasts and whole birds are done. An internal temperature reading of 160°F is considered the safe point in cooking, whereby any harmful bacteria are eliminated. Meats will continue cooking even after they leave the heat, so it is often possible to pull a roast off the fire when its internal temperature is 150° to 155°F and let it rest for a few minutes; its internal temperature will rise to 160°F.

Jerk Flavors

After years of studying culinary arts in Europe, I returned to Jamaica in 1969 to begin work as a hotel manager with my husband, Hartmut. We were asked to manage a wonderful resort called Goblin Hill in Portland. It was an idyllic setting, and we developed a reputation for having the finest food on that side of the island.

On our way to work each day we passed by a jerk stand—primitive, oh, so primitive—in Boston Beach. Now, you must remember that back then jerk cooking had none of the popularity it enjoys today.

One day, when I saw the jerk stand, I said to my husband, "Willinsky, let us re-create this whole feeling at the hotel—the jerk pork, the beer, the music, the people." So we instituted Sunday afternoon parties where we served rum punch and Boston Beach jerk to hotel guests.

Charles and Tony, our jerk experts, would prepare the seasoning the night before, using my Aunt Becky's finger-licking recipe. She had the most wonderful jerk spice combination, which she would pound in a mortar and slather over her pork and chicken. On Sunday, the meat was grilled in a billowing cloud of aromatic smoke. A piece of zinc roofing loosely covered the grill, capturing the smoke and helping to keep the meat moist. It is the aromatic flavor of smoke, combined with the secret combinations of spices, that captivates. Now, I will share with you some of my secret recipes.

JERK RUB

Makes about 1 cup; enough for 4 to 6 pounds of meat

DRY JERK SEASONING

Makes 5 tablespoons

Pastes made of spices, herbs, and onions are the most popular and authentic jerk flavoring method. The paste is rubbed all over the surface of the raw meat to add flavor. This is a medium-hot paste; it can be made hotter with the addition of more chilies or hot pepper sauce. If you want less heat, remove the seeds and ribs of the chilies before grinding them. Scotch bonnet or habanero chilies are preferred, but you can substitute the milder, more readily available jalapeño or serrano chilies.

....

1 onion, finely chopped
½ cup finely chopped scallions, including
   green parts
2 teaspoons fresh thyme leaves
2 teaspoons salt
1 teaspoon ground Jamaican allspice
¼ teaspoon ground nutmeg
½ teaspoon ground cinnamon
4 to 6 Scotch bonnet or habanero chilies,
   minced fine
1 teaspoon freshly ground black pepper

....

Using a mortar and pestle or a food processor, combine all the ingredients and grind to a paste. Store leftover paste in the refrigerator in a tightly closed jar for about 1 month.

This seasoning mix is excellent to have on hand to sprinkle on cooked or raw fish, vegetables, or snacks. It does not have quite as strong a flavor as the rub and marinade. To increase the heat, add more cayenne.

....

1 tablespoon onion flakes
1 tablespoon onion powder
2 teaspoons ground dried thyme
2 teaspoons salt
1 teaspoon ground Jamaican allspice
¼ teaspoon ground nutmeg
¼ teaspoon ground cinnamon
2 teaspoons sugar
1 teaspoon coarsely ground black pepper
1 teaspoon cayenne pepper
2 teaspoons dried chives or green onions

....

Mix together all the ingredients. Store leftover seasoning in a tightly closed glass jar. It will keep its pungency for over a month.

7

JERK MARINADE

Makes about 1½ cups; enough for about 4 pounds of meat

1 yellow onion, finely chopped
½ cup finely chopped scallions
2 teaspoons fresh thyme leaves
1 teaspoon salt
2 teaspoons sugar
1 teaspoon ground Jamaican
  allspice
½ teaspoon ground nutmeg
½ teaspoon ground cinnamon
1 habanero, jalapeño, or serrano
  chili, chopped
1 teaspoon freshly ground
  black pepper
3 tablespoons soy sauce
1 tablespoon vegetable oil
1 tablespoon cider vinegar or
  distilled white vinegar

Some people find marinades more convenient to use than spice pastes. This marinade is thicker than most marinades. The flavor may strike you as a bit harsh when you first make it, but I assure you, the flavors will blend and mellow as the meat cooks. To increase the heat of this rather mild marinade, add hot pepper sauce. If you want less heat, remove the seeds and ribs of the chilies before grinding them. This is an excellent marinade for chicken, beef, or pork.

In a blender or food processor, combine all the ingredients and process until smooth. Store leftover marinade in the refrigerator in a tightly closed jar for about 1 month.

Jamaican Ingredients

Most of the ingredients used in this cookbook are easily found in supermarkets across the country. Some are more likely to be found in stores that cater to a Latino clientele, and a few may need to be special-ordered. You will find sources for Jamaican ingredients in the back of this book. Here are some of the more common foods used in Jamaican cuisine.

BREADFRUIT

The breadfruit is a large, round, green, starchy fruit grown on enormous, elegant plants. The fruit has a pebbled green skin. Inside, the meat is white. One breadfruit can feed a whole family—baked, mashed, or boiled, just as you would a potato. The texture of breadfruit is lighter than that of a potato, however, more like bread. Breadfruit is usually roasted over hot coals and served with jerk pork or chicken. You can also bake breadfruit in your oven. Because of its size, it takes about two hours to bake.

Most Jamaicans' favorite variety of breadfruit is called Yellow Heart. The flesh is slightly sweet and it tastes and looks just like butter. This variety is a little difficult to find, but if you get the opportunity, buy it! Roast breadfruit and pear (avocado) served together (sliced, not mashed) is a real treat in Jamaica. If you can make it with a Yellow Heart and Simmons (a variety of avocado), you have heaven!

You can find fresh breadfruit in Spanish and West Indian markets. Treat it like a potato and store it in a cool, dry place. I do not peel breadfruit before baking it, but I do peel it for any other form of cooking.

CALLALOO

The green leaves of the taro plant, callaloo is a staple of Jamaican cooking. The leaves are cooked slow and long, like collards, or they are used in the extremely popular soup also called callaloo, which also contains seafood, pork, yams, okra, coconut milk, chilies, and lime. You can find it in Caribbean markets.

CHILIES

We Jamaicans like our food spicy hot. We use Scotch bonnet and bird chilies, also called Thai bird chilies. The medium-sized Scotch bonnet is a flavorful thick-skinned round pepper shaped like a bonnet; it may be red, yellow, or green. Habaneros are the best substitutes for Scotch bonnets. You can substitute jalapeño or serrano chilies, which are milder, if you must. Many recipes call for adding the chili whole and removing it after the dish is cooked. In this way, we get the flavor of the chili without the heat. If you want less heat, in recipes calling for sliced or ground chili, remove the seeds and the ribs from the chili before using it in the recipe.

In Jamaica, a fresh hot chili and a sharp knife are always served on the side of a plate so that the diner can sliver off pieces of chili as their palate allows.

Hot pepper sauces can always be used to spice up dishes. Scotch bonnet pepper sauce is preferred for most dishes and to add heat to the basic Jerk Marinade (page 8) and Jerk Rub (page 7). Pickapeppa Sauce is another Jamaican pepper sauce that can add heat to your food, as is Busha Browne's Pukka Hot Pepper Sauce. (Sources for companies that market Jamaican pepper sauces are listed at the back of this book.)

CHOCHO (CHAYOTE SQUASH)

Chocho is the Jamaican name for the bland, pear-shaped squash known as chayote to those of Spanish heritage and christophene to those of French origin. You might also encounter it under the names *mirliton* or *vegetable pear*. Botanists call it a "one-seeded cucumber;" you can substitute cucumber for chocho in some recipes.

If you have the choice, select the female chocho, which has a smooth, tender skin; the male chocho has a furrowed, prickly skin. Chocho is added to soups and stews, and can be puréed, stuffed, baked, creamed, or steamed.

COCONUTS

In Jamaica, nobody bothers with packages of sweetened dried coconut such as you see in the baking section of most U.S. supermarkets. We use fresh coconuts, and they are quite easy to prepare. Here are some helpful tips.

GRATING FRESH COCONUT: Take a large, ripe (brown) coconut without any cracks and containing liquid (shake it to hear the water sloshing). Pierce the eyes of the coconut with an ice pick or a skewer. Drain the liquid and reserve it for another use (especially Rum and Coconut Water, page 158).

Bake the coconut in a preheated 400°F oven for 15 minutes. This will cause the flesh to shrink from the shell and make it easier to remove. Break the coconut with a hammer and remove the flesh from the shell, flipping it out carefully with a strong knife. Peel off the brown membrane with a vegetable peeler. Cut the coconut meat into small pieces. In a blender or food processor, grind the pieces, a few at a time. (Or, grate the meat on the fine rasps of a box grater.) You should have about 4 cups.

MAKING FRESH COCONUT MILK: Put 2 cups of cubed fresh coconut in a blender or food processor fitted with the metal blade and process until smooth. Add 1½ cups very hot water and blend for 1 minute in the blender or 2 minutes in the food processor. Let cool for at least 5 minutes. Strain through a fine-meshed sieve lined with a double thickness of rinsed and squeezed cheesecloth, pressing hard on the solids with the back of a large spoon to extract as much liquid as you can. Bring the corners of the cheesecloth together and squeeze the remaining milk through the sieve into the bowl. Makes about 1½ cups.

In a pinch, you can make coconut milk from packaged sweetened flaked coconut. This yields a sweet milk that would be suitable for desserts but not for savory dishes.

Making fresh coconut milk is time-consuming. You can substitute unsweetened canned or frozen coconut milk, available in many supermarkets. Stores that cater to Asians, particularly Thais, and Latinos will always carry coconut milk.

Some of the recipes in this book call for cream of coconut. This sweetened coconut milk is available canned in most supermarkets. Look for the Goya or Coco López label. Sometimes cream of coconut is called piña colada mix. Do not substitute cream of coconut for coconut milk.

GINGER

Fresh Jamaican ginger is used in many recipes in that country. This is not quite the same fresh ginger root called for in many Chinese recipes. Jamaican ginger is very pungent and robust with dark skin; Chinese ginger has lighter skin and is fresher in flavor. The recipes in this book call for Chinese ginger; if you have access to Jamaican ginger (which is hard to find outside Jamaica), use a little less. Because ginger is so irregularly shaped, it is sometimes hard to measure it exactly. That's okay; exact measurements aren't important. In Jamaica, we usually measure ginger in terms of the hand. A whole root is called a hand; a "knuckle" is about the length of the knuckle of your finger: ¾ to 1 inch. A finger, as you can guess, is a finger-length piece about 3 inches long. A full hand of ginger is usually 4 to 6 inches long and with some "fingers" branching off from it.

GRENADINE SYRUP

Grenadine syrup is available commercially in the United States as well as Jamaica and gives a wonderful pink color to any concoction.

GUNGO PEAS / PIGEON PEAS

Gungo peas are a legume that came to the Caribbean from Africa, but they are now grown all over the world in tropical and subtropical regions (they are especially popular in India). In Jamaica, we cook them like beans and serve them with rice, or put them in soups. Usually, gungo peas are sold dried and split in Latino, Indian, and Caribbean markets, though you might also find them in regular supermarkets in the American South.

PIMENTO (JAMAICAN ALLSPICE)

Some cooks may think that allspice is a blend of cinnamon, nutmeg, and cloves because that is the aroma given off by the ground spice. But, in fact, allspice is the fruit of the pimento tree, which grows wild in the Caribbean. When Spanish explorers found the berries, they named the spice pimento, because the dried berries look like large peppercorns. Botanists named the tree *Pimenta officinalis*. So what we call pimento in Jamaica is called allspice in the States, and the spice is readily available in any supermarket, whole or ground.

Jamaican allspice, one of the key ingredients in jerk flavorings, is more pungent than allspice berries grown elsewhere. If you want true Jamaican flavor, then you must seek out a source for authentic Jamaican allspice. The oil content of the Jamaican berry is much higher, and that gives the spice its special flavor. Look for supermarket spice brands that specify Jamaican allspice.

PLANTAINS

The plantain is the big sister to the banana. It may be up to three times bigger than the standard Cavendish banana that everyone knows, thanks to the large companies like Dole and Chiquita.

We in the islands cannot live without plantains. They are eaten at every stage of maturity from green to ripe. In Jamaica, green plantains are fried and eaten as chips. We eat "turn" (partially ripe, or yellow) plantains boiled in soup. Ripe plantains, which are black in color and may look rotten to the uninformed, are either baked or fried and served as a side dish, or made into plantain tarts.

The greenish or yellow plantains that you will see in the supermarket are not fully ripe. No problem! Buy them as they are, take them home, and wrap them in newspaper for 4 to 5 days, by which time they should be much softer. Never put them in the refrigerator, as this will alter their flavor. Bake or fry them; that is island eating!

SWEET POTATOES

Latinos call sweet potatoes *boniatos* or *batatas*. Eaten in large quantities by both Latinos and Jamaicans, the skins of sweet potatoes range from pale yellowish orange to red to purplish brown in color. The paler ones are slightly sweet in taste and are almost powdery in texture after baking; the redder ones (sometimes erroneously called "yams" in the United States) are much sweeter and moister. In Jamaica, sweet potatoes are put to many and varied uses, including boiled and in soups and in the most wonderful desserts.

One, one coco full basket.

TAMARIND

The thirty-foot-tall tamarind tree yields a seedpod that contains a flavorful, acidic pulp that is used to flavor drinks and condiments. It is one of the key ingredients in Worcestershire sauce.

Tamarind pods are available in Latino and Asian markets. Middle Eastern food stores often carry the pulp in plastic-wrapped blocks. You can also find the drink in cans in the supermarket under the Goya label, among other brands.

YAMS

True yams are large edible roots that should not be confused with sweet potatoes. (What we call yams in the United States are really orange sweet potatoes.) Yams come in a variety of shapes and sizes. Their skins range in color from whitish to dark brown; the flesh may be whitish, pale yellow, pink, or purplish. My grandmother especially loved a variety called yellow yam that was the color of butter. She looked for yams that were very dry and waxy. Although not as common as sweet potatoes, yams can be found in the States, especially in produce markets that cater to Latino clientele.

With jerk chicken or pork, yams are usually left in their skins and baked over the same coals as the meat. But yams can also be peeled and boiled in soups or served mashed. As far as cooking, treat yams as you would sweet potatoes and you can't go wrong.

CHAPTER 2

PORK

Long before pigs were domesticated in Jamaica, Christopher Columbus discovered the Arawak Indians cooking small wild boars over hot coals buried deep in the ground. Later, the tradition of barbecuing pork was confined to Maroon Town, a village on the seventy-eight-hundred-foot-high Blue Mountains in the parish of Portland, the home of the former slaves known as Maroons. Over time, the Maroons lost their monopoly on barbecuing pork as others adopted the method, and gradually the practice of jerking found its way down the mountainside until it reached Boston Beach in Port Antonio. This beach is a well-known bathing strip a few miles out of Port Antonio, the capital of Portland. It is heavily frequented by people from Kingston, seventy miles away, as well as by a considerable number of tourists.

Undoubtedly, the best jerk on the island is made by a man who has a pit by the side of the road there. It is a corrugated zinc shed, open on all sides, in which two whole pigs are always being barbecued, from midmorning to night. The smell, the heat, the pungency, are marvelous. Devotees, most of them in bathing suits, stay all day. No matter how long it takes, they wait until the master says, "A' ready now," and begins to cut. "How much yo' want? Quarter pound, half pound?" and his long knife begins to slice through the tender meat.

They are devotees, indeed. So spicy is the meat, suffused with black pepper and Scotch bonnet chili, that it can hardly be eaten. The smallest taste is enough to make the eyes water. The palate can tolerate the fiery substance only after repeated attempts.

Boston Beach jerk pork is the most authentic jerk in Jamaica. There are other pits—in Ocho Rios, 60 miles away, in Montego Bay, a further 60, and in Negril, still a further 60, but it is acknowledged that they cannot rival the jerk of Boston Beach.

But if you cannot come to Boston Beach, you can still jerk pork in your own backyard!

Hog say, fus water 'im ketch, 'im walla.

BUTTERFLIED PORK LOIN ON THE GRILL

Serves 8 to 10

One 4-pound boneless pork roast
2 onions, finely chopped
1 tablespoon fresh thyme leaves
½ teaspoon ground Jamaican
   allspice
¼ teaspoon ground nutmeg
¼ teaspoon ground cinnamon
1 tablespoon sugar
2 tablespoons hot pepper sauce
¼ cup soy sauce
2 tablespoons vegetable oil

Crisp on the outside, tender and moist inside, this easy-to-prepare pork loin is perfect for parties. Serve it with Baked Sweet Potatoes (page 117) and Jamaican Cole Slaw (page 123). Or bury the sweet potatoes in the coals and roast them along with the meat!

Trim any excess fat from the pork roast. Butterfly the roast by cutting horizontally through the center almost to the end, then opening the meat up like a book. If in doubt, ask your butcher to butterfly it for you. The meat should lie flat. Place the pork in a shallow dish.

Combine the remaining ingredients to make a jerk paste. Spread the paste all over the pork loin, cover, and refrigerate for 4 to 6 hours. Let the chilled meat come to room temperature before grilling.

Prepare a medium-hot fire in a charcoal grill or preheat a gas grill to 350°F. If you are using a charcoal grill, when the coals have burned down, rake them to the side. Set a drip pan in the center of the grill and arrange the coals around it to provide indirect heat. If you're using a gas grill, place the drip pan away from the burner.

Place the pork on the grill over the pan. Cook for about 2 hours, turning the meat once, or until an instant-read thermometer inserted in the center of the meat registers 155° to 165°F.

Cut the butterflied pork loin in half lengthwise. Cut into thin slices and serve.

JAMAICAN JERK BARBECUED RIBS
Serves 4

1 cup Jerk Marinade (page 8)
1 tablespoon sugar
2 tablespoons red wine vinegar
4 pounds pork spareribs
About 1½ cups barbecue sauce, commercial or homemade (page 47)

In this recipe, jerk flavors are combined with barbecue sauce. The sauce, added during the final 15 minutes of cooking, adds a delicious crust to the succulent ribs. Any store-bought barbecue sauce will do, or you can make your own. Serve these with Rice and Peas (page 120) and a salad. Add lots of brightly colored napkins, Jamaican Red Stripe beer, and reggae music.

Combine the Jerk Marinade, sugar, and vinegar. Add the ribs and turn to coat lightly. Marinate in the refrigerator for 4 to 6 hours. Let the chilled meat come to room temperature before grilling.

Prepare a low fire in a charcoal grill or preheat a gas grill to 225°F. If you're using a charcoal grill, when the coals have burned down, rake them to the side. Set a drip pan in the center of the fuel bed and arrange the coals around it to provide indirect heat. If you're using a gas grill, place the drip pan away from the burner. Place the ribs on the grill over the drip pan, cover the grill, and cook for 4 to 5 hours, turning and brushing frequently with the marinade. Add more coals as needed during the cooking time to keep the fire at an even 225°F. Brush the ribs with the barbecue sauce during the last 15 minutes of cooking.

GLAZED SPARERIBS
Serves 6

About 6 pounds pork spareribs
½ cup Jerk Marinade (page 8)
2 cups apple jelly or other
  fruit jelly
1 cup water
1 teaspoon curry powder

A two-part cooking process makes these ribs especially tender.

Place the spareribs in a shallow dish, coat them with the Jerk Marinade, and refrigerate for 2 to 4 hours. Allow the chilled ribs to come to room temperature before cooking.

Preheat the oven to 350°F. Arrange the marinated spareribs, meaty side down, on a baking sheet with sides or a roasting pan. Bake for 1 hour, turning once if needed. This part of the preparation can be done the day before. (Alternatively, prepare a low fire in a charcoal grill or preheat a gas grill to 225°F and cook the ribs, covered, for 2 to 3 hours.)

Prepare a medium fire in a charcoal grill or preheat a gas grill to 350°F. (If you cooked the ribs over a low/225°F fire to begin with, remove the ribs from the grill while you replenish the coals and rake them together to increase the heat to medium, or preheat the gas grill to 350°F).

In a small saucepan, make the glaze by combining the apple jelly, water, and curry powder. Bring to a boil. Reduce the heat to low and cook, stirring, for about 3 minutes. Remove from the heat and keep warm.

Put the ribs on the grill, meaty side up. Spread the glaze lightly over the ribs. Cook for 10 to 15 minutes, or until the bottom is crisp. Turn and glaze lightly again. Continue cooking until nicely browned on the second side. Coat again with the glaze after removing from the grill. Serve hot.

JERKED ASIAN SPARERIBS
Serves 4

4 pounds pork spareribs
2 teaspoons salt
2 tablespoons sugar
⅓ cup rice wine or dry sherry
⅓ cup soy sauce
3 tablespoons Jerk Rub (page 7)

Asian foods are very popular in Jamaica. This delicious recipe for spareribs uses rice wine and soy sauce. You can bake these ribs in the oven or grill them on a barbecue grill.

Cut the pork into individual ribs. In a shallow ovenproof dish, combine the remaining ingredients and stir until smooth. Add the ribs, turn them to coat, then cover and refrigerate for 2 to 4 hours, turning once or twice. Bring the chilled meat to room temperature before cooking.

Preheat the oven or gas grill to 400°F or prepare a hot fire in a charcoal grill.

Bake the ribs for 40 to 45 minutes, or until tender, turning and basting once halfway through. Or, barbecue the ribs on a grill for 20 to 25 minutes, until browned, basting and turning once. Serve hot.

PORK-PINEAPPLE KABOBS

Serves 4 (2 skewers per person)

One 1½-pound boneless pork loin,
cut in 1½- to 2-inch cubes
¾ cup Jerk Marinade (page 8)
1 fresh pineapple, peeled, cored,
and cut into 2-inch cubes
2 green bell peppers, seeded,
deribbed, and cut into 2-inch
squares
12 pearl onions, peeled, or 1 large
yellow onion, peeled and cut
into 1-inch wedges

The fresh fruit adds a wonderful, sweet flavor to these kabobs.

In a resealable plastic bag, combine the pork and jerk marinade. Rotate the bag several times to coat the meat with the marinade. Refrigerate for 2 to 4 hours.

Prepare a hot fire in a charcoal grill. Meanwhile, add the pineapple and vegetables to the meat and marinade. At the same time, soak 8 wooden skewers in water for 20 to 30 minutes.

Skewer the pork and vegetables alternately on the skewers. Grill for about 15 to 20 minutes, turning to brown the meat on all sides and basting with the marinade. Serve hot.

ROASTED PORK

Serves 8 to 10

2 cloves garlic, finely chopped
¼ cup soy sauce
1 Scotch bonnet, habanero, or
   jalapeño chili, minced, or
     1 tablespoon hot pepper sauce
½ teaspoon dried thyme
½ teaspoon ground Jamaican
   allspice
1 boneless pork loin roast
   (3 to 4 pounds)

This pork is roasted in the oven, but the flavor is typical of jerk cooking. I like to serve it with Honey-Ginger Dipping Sauce (page 127). You will need to start this recipe the day before serving.

Mix together the garlic, soy sauce, chili, thyme, and pimento. Using a small knife, pierce the pork all over. Rub the spice mixture into the meat. Cover and refrigerate overnight.

Preheat the oven to 350°F. Place the meat in a roasting pan and loosely cover with aluminum foil. Roast for 1 hour, and then uncover and continue roasting for 10 to 40 minutes (20 to 25 minutes total per pound), or until an instant-read thermometer inserted in the center of the pork registers 155° to 165°F. Transfer the pork to a platter and let stand for 10 minutes before carving.

ROASTED PORK TENDERLOIN

Serves 4

2 tablespoons finely chopped
    scallion greens
1 teaspoon fresh thyme leaves
1 teaspoon salt
¼ teaspoon ground Jamaican
    allspice
Pinch of ground nutmeg
Pinch of ground cinnamon
2 teaspoons hot pepper sauce
1 tablespoon soy sauce
1 teaspoon sugar
Two pork tenderloins,
    trimmed (1½ to 2 pounds total
    untrimmed weight)

Another roasted pork recipe for those who can't barbecue year-round. I like to serve this with Tamarind-Apricot Sauce (page 128) with the optional mustard added. Pork tenderloins are quick cooking and very tender. Serve with Baked Sweet Potatoes (page 117) or Fried Plantains (page 116) and a salad.

Preheat the oven to 350°F.

Combine all the ingredients, except the pork, to make a jerk paste. Place the tenderloin in a baking dish and smear the jerk paste all over it. Roast for 30 to 45 minutes, or until an instant-read thermometer inserted in the center registers 150° to 160°F. The meat will be cooked through but still juicy. Slice the meat against the grain and serve.

1½ tablespoons Dry Jerk
Seasoning (page 7) or
Walkerswood Jerk Seasoning
2 tablespoons grated fresh ginger
1 tablespoon minced garlic
1 teaspoon salt
One 2-pound piece pork loin
or boneless pork shoulder,
butterflied
2 yellow plantains with black
flecks, peeled
1 tablespoon tamarind pulp
1 tablespoon honey
1 tablespoon olive oil
Fruit chutney, preferably
Walkerswood Sorrel Chutney,
for serving

This recipe is from the brilliant cook Virginia Burke of the Walkerswood Company. It's a contemporary take on traditional jerk pork, and each slice contains a round of plantain, which is both a good accompaniment and a fun presentation. As always, adjust the amount of jerk seasoning to your taste. Have your butcher butterfly the pork for you.

In a small bowl, combine the jerk seasoning, ginger, garlic, and salt. Stir to blend. Rub the pork all over with this mixture, then place the pork in a baking dish, cover, and refrigerate overnight.

Preheat the oven to 350°F. Open the pork flat and pound it with a mallet or roll flat with a rolling pin. Cut the plantains to fit and lay them lengthwise in the slit. Close the pork around the plantain and tie in several places with kitchen twine to secure the roll.

Place the pork in a roasting pan. In a small bowl, mix the tamarind pulp, honey, and olive oil together. Brush some of this mixture over the pork. Cover the pork loosely with aluminum foil and roast for 1 hour. Remove the foil and roast, occasionally brushing the pork with more tamarind mixture, for 30 to 40 minutes, or until an instant-read thermometer inserted into the meat (but not into the plantain) registers 160°F. Remove from the oven and let rest, covered with foil, for 10 minutes. Cut the pork into slices and serve with the chutney alongside.

JAMAICAN JERK PORK
Serves 6 to 8

6 tablespoons Dry Jerk Seasoning (page 7) or Busha Browne's Jerk Seasoning

1 tablespoon hot pepper sauce, preferably Busha Browne's Pukka Hot Pepper Sauce

2-inch piece fresh ginger, peeled and grated

6 cloves garlic, minced

1½ teaspoons salt

¼ cup canola oil

1 pork shoulder (pork butt), 6 to 8 pounds

This classic jerk recipe is from the wonderful Winston Stona of the Busha Browne company, which makes some of the best Jamaican food products.

In a small bowl, combine the jerk seasoning, hot sauce, ginger, garlic, salt, and oil. Stir to blend. Rub this marinade into the pork, place in a dish, cover, and refrigerate overnight.

Prepare a low fire in a charcoal grill, or preheat a gas grill to 225°F. Oil the grill grate. Remove the pork from the refrigerator, reserving the marinade. Let the meat come to room temperature before grilling. Meanwhile, bring the reserved marinade to a boil in a small saucepan. Set aside.

If you are using a charcoal grill, when the coals have burned down, rake them to the side. Set a drip pan in the center of the grill and arrange the coals around it to provide indirect heat. If you're using a gas grill, place the drip pan away from the burner.

Place the pork on the grill over the pan. Cook for about 6 to 8 hours, replenishing the fuel as necessary to keep the fire at 225°F and basting occasionally with the reserved marinade, or until an instant-read thermometer inserted in the center of the meat registers 160°F. You will be able to easily pull the large bone out of the shoulder—the pork is definitely done when you can do this. Allow the pork to cool, then with large forks, pull the pork apart into shreds, or you can chop the pork with a cleaver. Serve on a platter with rolls.

ASIAN-STYLE ROAST PORK
Serves 4

2 tablespoons soy sauce
1 teaspoon light or dark rum
2 tablespoons catsup
2 teaspoons Jerk Rub (page 7)
3 tablespoons chicken broth
1 tablespoon sugar
One 1½-pound pork tenderloin, trimmed
1¼ cups Honey-Ginger Dipping Sauce (page 127)

This pork is marinated with ingredients people think of when they think of Jamaica (rum, jerk seasonings), but it's roasted and served with a Chinese-style dipping sauce that's also very Jamaican, due to the Asian influences on our cooking. Serve this with steamed rice.

In a small, deep dish just large enough to hold the pork, combine the soy sauce, rum, catsup, jerk rub, chicken broth, and sugar. Mix thoroughly. Add the pork, turning it to coat it with the marinade. Cover and refrigerate for 3 to 6 hours. Remove from the refrigerator 30 minutes before roasting.

Preheat the oven to 350°F. Place the pork on a rack set in a roasting pan and roast for 35 minutes. Pour ¾ cup of the dipping sauce over the pork roast and roast for an additional 10 minutes, or until an instant-read thermometer inserted in the center of the meat registers 155° to 165°F. Transfer the meat to a cutting board and let stand for 10 minutes. Carve the pork against the grain into thin slices and arrange on a warmed platter. Serve with the remaining Honey-Ginger Dipping Sauce alongside.

JERK ROASTED SUCKLING PIG

Serves 12 to 15

JERK PASTE

4 onions, finely chopped

2 cups finely chopped scallions, including pale green parts

4 tablespoons dried thyme

¼ cup salt

2 tablespoons ground Jamaican allspice

¼ teaspoon ground nutmeg

1 teaspoon ground cinnamon

2 to 4 habanero or Scotch bonnet chilies, seeded

1 tablespoon freshly ground black pepper

½ cup vegetable oil

6 cloves garlic

1 suckling pig (about 10 pounds), dressed and well cleaned

Vegetable oil for coating

Salt and freshly ground pepper for sprinkling

2 or 3 baked potatoes, peeled and mashed

2 or 3 baked sweet potatoes, peeled and mashed

2 or 3 tablespoons unsalted butter

Roasted suckling pig is one of the dishes that is served when Jamaicans entertain lavishly for large gatherings at weddings, hotel buffets, Christmas parties, and New Year's Eve parties. Generally, it is prepared and brought in by someone who specializes in "roast pig." Traditionally, a suckling pig is roasted on a spit over a wood fire, but if you have a large enough oven, you can prepare one at home. Serve it with Baked Plantains (page 116) and Baked Breadfruit (page 115).

Preheat the oven to 350°F. In a food processor, puree all the paste ingredients to make a paste. Rub the inside of the pig with the paste, reserving 1 tablespoon to mix with the stuffing. Rub the outside of the pig with oil, salt, and pepper.

In a large bowl, combine the potatoes, sweet potatoes, butter, and remaining 1 tablespoon jerk paste; stir until well blended. Loosely pack the stuffing inside the pig and close the opening with skewers or sew together with kitchen twine. Draw the legs back and tie with kitchen twine. Stuff the mouth with a piece of aluminum foil to keep it open as the pig roasts.

Place the pig on a rack in a large roasting pan. Roast for 2 to 2½ hours (15 minutes per pound). When done, an instant-read thermometer inserted in the thigh will register 165°F, and the juices will run clear when the thigh is pierced.

Remove the pig from the oven and place on a warmed platter. Remove the foil from the mouth and replace it with an apple. Let the pig rest for 10 to 15 minutes before carving.

1 tablespoon Dry Jerk Seasoning
  (page 7)
2 pounds boneless pork loin chops
2 tablespoons vegetable oil
2 large firm apples, peeled, cored,
  and sliced ½ inch thick
Tamarind-Apricot Sauce (page
  128), prepared with the optional
  mustard

Boneless pork loin chops are fast cooking and relatively inexpensive since there is no bone or other waste. You can make this a complete meal by adding sweet potato slices to the pork and apples. This is wonderful with Jamaican Cole Slaw (page 123).

Rub the jerk seasoning all over the pork. In a large skillet, heat the oil over medium-high heat. Add the meat and cook until browned, about 3 minutes on each side. Reduce the heat to low and place the apple slices on top of the meat. Cover and cook for 10 minutes, or until the apples are soft.

Pour 3 tablespoons of the Tamarind-Apricot Sauce over the pork and the apples to make a glaze. Cook, uncovered, for 1 more minute, then turn both the apples and the meat and cook on the other side for 1 more minute. Serve with the remaining sauce alongside and the pan drippings poured over.

JERK PORK CHOPS
AND PINEAPPLE RICE PILAF

Serves 4

4 lean, center-cut pork chops,
    about ½ inch thick
4 teaspoons Dry Jerk Seasoning
    (page 7)
3 tablespoons vegetable oil
¾ cup long-grain white rice
4 scallions, including green parts,
    chopped (keep white and green
    parts separate)
1 cup chicken broth
2 teaspoons fresh lime juice
1 cup ½-inch diced fresh
    pineapple

Pork, pineapple, and jerk- and lime-seasoned rice make an easy-to-prepare meal with a Jamaican twist. Serve with a salad.

Preheat the oven to 350°F. Sprinkle the chops on both sides with 2 teaspoons of the dry jerk seasoning. In a large ovenproof skillet, heat the oil over medium-high heat and cook the chops until browned, about 3 minutes on each side. Transfer the chops to a plate. Add the rice and white part of the scallions to the pan. Stir in the remaining 2 teaspoons jerk seasoning. Sauté, stirring constantly, until the grains of rice are golden brown, about 5 minutes.

Stir the broth and lime juice into the rice. Place the chops on top of the rice. Cover and bake for 20 minutes. Stir in the fruit and green scallion tops. Taste and adjust the seasoning. Re-cover and continue baking for 15 minutes, or until the rice and the chops are tender. Fluff the rice lightly with a fork and serve.

PORK AND MANGO CURRY

Serves 6

3 tablespoons all-purpose flour

One 1½-pound pork tenderloin, cut into 1-inch cubes

2 tablespoons vegetable oil

1 onion, thickly sliced

2 small red or green bell peppers, seeded, deribbed, and sliced

1 tablespoon curry powder

2 tablespoons Dry Jerk Seasoning (page 7) or to taste

1 knuckle (1-inch cube) fresh ginger, peeled and grated

One 16-ounce can peeled tomatoes, with juice

2 teaspoons tomato paste

1½ cups chicken broth

1½ pounds boiling potatoes, peeled and cubed

2 large ripe mangoes, peeled, pitted, and sliced

Curried foods came to Jamaica along with the East Indians who were brought there in the mid-1800s as indentured servants. This dish combines jerk seasoning and curry powder. Serve with steamed rice, chutney, and fried plantains.

Put the flour in a plastic bag and add the pork cubes. Toss to coat the meat with the flour.

In a Dutch oven, heat the oil over medium-high heat. Add the pork and sauté for about 5 minutes, or until lightly browned. Add the onion and bell peppers and sauté for 3 more minutes. Stir in the curry, dry jerk seasoning, and ginger. Cook, stirring constantly, for 1 minute. Add the tomatoes with their juice, tomato paste, broth, and potatoes. Stir well, reduce the heat to low, and cook for 20 to 25 minutes. Stir in the mango slices, remove from heat, and serve in bowls.

SMOKED FRESH HAM

Serves 12 to 14

1 fresh bone-in ham, Boston
   butt, or pork shoulder (6 to
   8 pounds)
Jerk Rub (page 7)
2 cups dry white wine
One 46-ounce can unsweetened
   pineapple juice
½ cup fresh lemon juice

If you use a Boston butt or pork shoulder, the meat will be similar to American pulled pork. This dish is wonderful with traditional American accompaniments: deviled eggs, baked beans, potato salad, and corn on the cob. Jamaican accompaniments would be Baked Breadfruit (page 115) and a mango salad. Smoked meat freezes very well. When I go to the effort to stoke up the smoker, I usually fill it with as much meat as I can.

Evenly coat the meat with the jerk rub. Mix the wine, pineapple juice, and lemon juice together and set aside.

Prepare a charcoal fire in an outdoor smoker and let it burn for 10 to 15 minutes, or heat an electric or gas smoker to 225°F. Place the water pan in the smoker and fill with the pineapple juice mixture. Add enough hot water to fill the pan if necessary.

Place the food in the smoker according to the manufacturer's directions. Cover with the smoker lid and cook for about 3½ hours. Remove the lid and turn the meat. Baste with drippings from the drip pan. If necessary, add more liquid to the drip pan. Cover again and continue to cook for 3 to 4 hours, or until very tender, with an internal temperature of 160°F.

Serve hot, if you can. Many people say smoked ham is not as good reheated and that leftovers should be served at room temperature. The meat can be sliced or pulled apart.

CHAPTER 3

CHICKEN AND FOWL

When I was a little girl in Jamaica, Sunday dinner was often a roast chicken that was laced with cracked pimentos and scallions. At that time we did not know the flavoring combination was jerk! But we loved it.

And my, those chickens were tasty—not like the poorly flavored supermarket chickens available these days. You see, every year for Easter, my grandma Hulda, who was raised in the country, gave each grandchild half a dozen multicolored chickens to raise. Then Grandma Hulda would bring another half dozen hens to the laying coop as well. Every morning, we would go out and pick the warm eggs from our own chickens. When the hens became too old to lay, they became Sunday dinner in some form—a roast, a delicious chicken fricassee, or soup.

So we all grew up with chicken—except for when a mongoose got in the coop and killed the chickens. Mongooses were brought from India or Africa to the sugar plantations to keep the snakes out, but they later became quite a nuisance as they multiplied and multiplied. It became quite a feat for my grandmother to figure out how to keep the mongooses from her chickens. Mesh wire was everywhere. She would even lay traps for the mongooses; Grandma Hulda was a tough old lady, I tell you!

It's no wonder we Jamaicans have invented so many jerk chicken recipes; chickens are less expensive and easier to raise than pigs, and they're very delicious when marinated and cooked in the jerk style. This chapter contains a variety of traditional and updated chicken recipes cooked jerk style. For a twist, I've also included a recipe for jerk Cornish hens in this chapter, and a couple of recipes for tropical chicken salads, perfect for entertaining.

Chicken deh merry, hawk deh near.

AUTHENTIC JAMAICAN JERK CHICKEN

Serves 6

2 chickens (about 3½ pounds
each), cut into serving pieces
3 cups Jerk Marinade (page 8)

For simplicity and authentic flavor, chicken marinated in jerk spices and cooked slow over a charcoal and wood fire can't be beat—though if you have a gas grill, never fear: it's still amazingly good.

Put the chicken in a large dish and pour over 2 cups of the marinade. Turn the chicken pieces over to coat them completely, cover, and refrigerate for 4 to 6 hours.

For authentic flavor, build a low fire in a charcoal grill with a combination of charcoal and pimento wood and hold the temperature around 225° F. If you don't have pimento wood, substitute apple wood or hickory, or use all charcoal. If using a gas grill, preheat to 225° to 250°F. Place the chicken pieces on the grill, skin side down. This will grease the grill and prevent the chicken from sticking. Cover the grill and cook the chicken, basting frequently with the remaining ¾ cup marinade and turning the chicken every 10 minutes or so, for 1½ to 2 hours. The chicken is done when the flesh feels firm and the juices run clear when the meat is pricked with a fork, and the internal temperature is 160°F.

DAVID'S JERK CHICKEN
Serves 6

½ cup Jerk Rub (page 7)
1 onion, finely chopped
1 habanero or Scotch bonnet chili,
 minced, or 2 tablespoons hot
 pepper sauce (optional)
Leaves from 1 fresh thyme sprig,
 minced
2 scallions, including green parts,
 finely chopped
1 chicken (3 to 3½ pounds),
 cut into serving pieces

In the parish of St. Ann, the garden parish of Jamaica, live my very good friends David and Eli Rickham, owners of a wonderful pimento plantation, Sussex Estate. Their home is way up on a rugged hilltop surrounded by acres and acres of pimento trees, which yield the main ingredient in jerk seasoning, with a magnificent view of the harbor. I have been there many times for Sunday lunch, a big event in Jamaica, and enjoyed David's jerk chicken.

David's chicken is cooked over an open fire of charcoal and pimento wood with the grill grate 1½ feet above the fire. But you can re-create his recipe by using a charcoal or gas grill. It's nice and spicy, so omit the fresh chili or hot pepper sauce if you like a milder flavor.

Mix together the jerk seasoning, onion, chili or hot pepper sauce, thyme, and scallions. Rub the chicken well all over with the jerk rub. Cover and refrigerate for 4 to 6 hours.

Prepare a low fire in a charcoal grill using a combination of charcoal and pimento wood. If you don't have pimento wood, substitute applewood or hickory, or build a fire with just charcoal. If you are using a gas grill, preheat it to 225° to 250°F.

Place the chicken on the grill and cook, covered, for 1 to 1½ hours, turning every 10 minutes or so. When it's done, the chicken will take on a very dark color, the juices will run clear when the meat is pierced, and the internal temperature will have reached 160°F.

JAMAICAN JERK CHICKEN BREASTS

Serves 4

4 large bone-in, skin-on chicken
 breast halves
2 to 3 teaspoons Jerk Rub
 (page 7)

White meat has a tendency to dry out on the grill, so these breasts are first baked slowly in the oven. Then they are finished on the grill to give them a crisp coating.

....

Smear the chicken with the jerk rub (apply a thin coating for medium spiciness, a thick coating for hotter flavor). Place in a buttered baking dish, cover, and refrigerate for 2 to 3 hours.

Preheat the oven to 275°F. Cover the dish with aluminum foil and bake the breasts for 30 minutes. Meanwhile, prepare a medium fire in a charcoal grill or preheat a gas grill to 250° to 275°F. Remove the breasts from the oven and immediately place them on the grill, skin side down. Grill for 5 minutes on each side, or until the skin is crisp.

BARBECUED CHICKEN

Serves 4

½ cup vegetable oil

1 cup cider vinegar

2 tablespoons Dry Jerk Seasoning
(page 7), plus more to taste

¼ teaspoon ground white pepper

1 large egg

4 large bone-in, skin-on chicken
breast halves

This barbecue sauce offers just the suggestion of jerk flavor. For more spice, generously sprinkle more dry jerk seasoning over the chicken as it cools. I like to serve this with Jamaican Cole Slaw (page 123) and French fries sprinkled with Dry Jerk Seasoning (page 7).

Prepare a low fire in a charcoal grill using a combination of charcoal and pimento wood. If you don't have pimento wood, substitute applewood or hickory, or use just charcoal. Or preheat a gas grill to 225° to 275°F.

In a blender, combine the oil, vinegar, the 2 tablespoons seasoning, the white pepper, and egg to make the barbecue sauce. Set aside.

Place the chicken on the grill, skin side down, and grill for 20 minutes, basting frequently with the sauce. Repeat on the second side, grilling for 20 minutes, or until the juices run clear when the meat is pierced. For more flavor, sprinkle generously with additional dry jerk seasoning after cooking.

JERK CORNISH HENS

Serves 4

4 Cornish hens (1½ pounds each)
2 tablespoons vegetable oil
3 tablespoons Dry Jerk Seasoning
  (page 7)
Honey-Ginger Dipping Sauce
  (page 127)

Dry jerk seasoning adds spark to the delicate flavor of Cornish hens, and the honey-ginger dipping sauce sweetens them up.

....

Prepare a medium fire in a charcoal grill or preheat a gas grill to 350°F. Meanwhile, soak 8 wooden skewers in water to cover.

Place each hen breast side down on a cutting board and remove its backbone by hitting the backbone hard with the flat side of a large knife or cleaver, then pressing down firmly to crack the bone. Then flatten the bird with your hand and cut away the backbone by making a cut on either side of the backbone with the knife or with kitchen scissors and pull to remove it. Cut away any protruding rib bones. Spread the halves out and press down on the breastbone to flatten. Insert 1 skewer through the wings and breast and 1 skewer through the legs of each bird to keep them flat.

Coat the hens all over with the oil, then with the jerk seasoning. Place them on the grill, skin side down. Cook, brushing the hens with some of the dipping sauce and turning them 2 to 3 times, for 15 to 20 minutes, or until the juices run clear when the meat is pierced. Serve hot, passing additional dipping sauce at the table.

JERK CHICKEN "HASH"

Serves 4

2 tablespoons vegetable oil

1 pound potatoes, cut into
  ¼-inch cubes

1 yellow onion, diced into
  ¼-inch pieces

3 cloves garlic, minced

1 tomato, diced

1 pound skinless, boneless chicken
  thighs, cut into bite-size pieces

2 tablespoons Dry Jerk Seasoning
  (page 7)

1 teaspoon ground cumin

2 tablespoons sesame seeds

½ cup chicken broth

3 scallions, including green
  parts, sliced

I usually make this for a hearty breakfast if there happens to be some leftover jerk chicken. You can use any chicken meat that you may have, but chicken thighs have a richer flavor and are worth "jerking" for just this recipe. You might top the chicken hash with your favorite grated cheese. Simple scrambled eggs with a side of sliced mango will make this a memorable breakfast.

Heat the oil in a large skillet or sauté pan over medium heat. Add the potatoes, onion, garlic, and tomato, stir all together, and cook for about 10 minutes. Add the chicken, stir in the jerk seasoning, cumin, and sesame seeds and continue to cook, stirring occasionally, for 3 to 5 minutes. Pour in the chicken broth and bring it to a boil. Reduce the heat to low and simmer, covered, until the liquid is absorbed, about 10 minutes. Remove from the heat and toss the chopped scallions over the chicken hash. Serve immediately.

CARIBBEAN ROASTED CHICKEN
Serves 4

One 3½-pound chicken
6 teaspoons Dry Jerk Seasoning
  (page 7)
½ cup Honey-Ginger Dipping
  Sauce (page 127)

A great low-fat way to cook chicken is to use a vertical roaster, which is available at most kitchen supply stores. This method makes a crisper chicken, since it allows all the fat to drain out. The chicken cooks faster, too, because it is in a freestanding, vertical position. But you can also cook this chicken in a roasting pan.

Remove all but one rack from your oven, and place that rack on the lowest rack setting. Preheat the oven to 350°F. Rub the cavity of the chicken with 2 teaspoons of dry jerk seasoning. Use your finger or the point of a knife to loosen the chicken skin over the breast and spread 2 more teaspoons of the seasoning directly over the breast of the chicken under the skin. Rub the remaining 2 teaspoons of the seasoning over the exterior of the chicken.

Place the chicken on the vertical roaster, if using, and place the roaster in a roasting pan to catch the drips. Roast for 45 minutes, or until the juices run clear when the thigh is pierced with a knife. If you are not using a vertical roaster, roast the chicken breast side up on a horizontal wire rack placed over a roasting pan for about 1¼ hours (20 minutes per pound), until the juices run clear when the thigh is pierced with a knife.

Cut the chicken into serving pieces, then drizzle each piece with some of the dipping sauce. Serve hot.

ISLAND GLAZED CHICKEN
Serves 4

1 chicken (3 to 4 pounds)
1 tablespoon Jerk Rub (page 7)
1 cup Passion Fruit Sauce
   (page 152)

Who would ever have thought that passion fruit would go with jerk seasoning? I assure you, it is great; the sweet and tangy passion fruit sauce balances the fiery flavor of the jerk.

Split the chicken down the back and flatten. Rub the meat on both sides with the jerk rub. Refrigerate for at least 1 hour or up to 4 hours.

Preheat the oven to 375°F, then roast the chicken in a roasting pan, uncovered, for 45 minutes. Pour the passion fruit sauce over the chicken and continue roasting for 30 minutes, or until the juices run clear when a thigh is pierced with a knife. Cut into serving pieces and serve.

SIMMERED JERK CHICKEN
Serves 4

1 cup water

½ cup soy sauce

2 tablespoons sugar

2 tablespoons rum or dry sherry

2 onions, chopped

¼ teaspoon aniseeds (optional)

4 teaspoons Dry Jerk Seasoning
(page 7), or 2 teaspoons Jerk
Rub (page 7)

1 chicken (3 to 4 pounds), skinned
and cut into serving pieces

One 4-ounce can sliced water
chestnuts, drained

I've been cooking this dish for over twenty years; it is a favorite of my children. Not only is it delicious, it also freezes very well. Serve this with steamed rice.

In a Dutch oven, combine the water, soy sauce, sugar, rum or sherry, onions, and aniseeds, if using, and bring to a boil. Stir in the jerk seasoning or rub, then add the chicken. The mixture should barely cover the chicken. Bring to a boil, then reduce the heat to a simmer. Cover and cook for 15 to 20 minutes. Turn the chicken over, re-cover, and cook for about 20 minutes more, or until the chicken is opaque throughout and the juices run clear when a piece of chicken is pierced with a knife. Add the water chestnuts and cook, uncovered, for 1 or 2 minutes. Skim off the fat. Serve hot.

BAKED JERK CHICKEN WINGS

Serves 4 as an appetizer, 2 to 3 as a main course

18 whole chicken wings, or
  12 drumsticks
1½ cups Jerk Marinade (page 8)
1½ cups Tamarind-Apricot
  Sauce (page 128)
¼ cup soy sauce

This dish is a delicious variation on Buffalo wings—spicy, and served with a very "morish" dipping sauce.

In a baking dish, combine the chicken and 1 cup of the marinade. Cover and refrigerate for at least 1½ hours or up to 4 hours, turning occasionally. The longer the chicken marinates, the hotter it becomes. Remove the chicken from the marinade and discard the marinade.

Preheat the oven to 350°F. Place the chicken in a greased baking dish. Bake for 40 to 45 minutes, basting twice with the reserved ½ cup of marinade. When done, the juices will run clear when the chicken is pierced with a knife.

Prepare a dipping sauce by combining the Tamarind-Apricot Sauce with the soy sauce. Serve the chicken hot or at room temperature, with the dipping sauce.

JERK CHICKEN STIR-FRY
Serves 4

¼ cup teriyaki sauce

2 tablespoons water

1 tablespoon dry sherry or
   Chinese Shaoxing wine

1 teaspoon cornstarch

2 tablespoons vegetable oil

1 pound boneless, skinless chicken
   breasts, cut into 1½-inch pieces

1 medium onion, chopped

2 teaspoons Dry Jerk Seasoning
   (page 7), or more to taste

¼ cup green peas

Because of immigration, Chinese cuisine has deep roots in Jamaican culture. This dish uses a classic technique of Chinese cooking to make a quick jerk chicken meal. Serve this with steamed rice.

In a small bowl, combine the teriyaki sauce, water, sherry or wine, and cornstarch. Whisk to blend.

In a wok or a large skillet, heat the oil over medium-high heat. Add the chicken and onion and stir-fry until the chicken is slightly browned and the onion is just golden, about 5 minutes. Season to taste with the dry jerk seasoning. Add the peas, then the teriyaki sauce mix. Cook until the sauce has thickened slightly, 5 to 8 minutes. Serve hot.

CARIBBEAN CHICKEN SALAD

Serves 6

3 whole, skin-on chicken breasts
2 tablespoons Jerk Marinade
  (page 8)
½ cup chopped celery
1 cup ½-inch diced fresh
  pineapple
2 tablespoons mayonnaise
2 cups finely shredded lettuce

Plan ahead and save yourself a little preparation time. If you are already grilling other items, cook some extra chicken breasts on the grill with jerk seasoning and use them later in this delicious salad.

Preheat the oven to 350°F. Arrange the chicken breasts, skin side up, in a roasting pan and pour the marinade over them. Bake for 20 to 25 minutes, or until opaque throughout. Remove from the oven and cool.

Cut or shred the chicken breasts into small pieces and put into a medium bowl. Stir in the celery, pineapple, and mayonnaise. Serve on a bed of lettuce. You can serve at once, but I prefer this salad well chilled.

SPICY CHICKEN SALAD IN A PINEAPPLE SHELL

Serves 2

1 pineapple
¼ cup Jerk Marinade (page 8)
¼ cup Honey-Ginger Dipping
  Sauce (page 127)
1 teaspoon vegetable oil
1 tablespoon chopped scallion
12 ounces boneless chicken
  breasts or thighs, broiled or
  grilled, then diced
¼ cup coarsely chopped roasted
  cashews

For festive occasions, this chicken salad looks smashing in its pineapple shell.

Slice the pineapple in half lengthwise. Cut out the tough core, then scoop out the flesh with a large, sturdy spoon, reserving the flesh and the shells. Dice the flesh.

In a large bowl, combine the marinade, dipping sauce, oil, and scallion. Add the diced chicken, diced pineapple, and cashews. Stir well until evenly coated. Serve the salad in the pineapple shells.

You may serve the salad at once, but I prefer to serve it well chilled.

CHAPTER 4

SEAFOOD

Fish has always been an important part of the Jamaican diet. But it must be *fresh, fresh* fish, as it was when I was growing up and refrigerators were small and freezers were definitely not part of the Jamaican household.

Buying fish was always an experience. My father and I would drive out about twenty miles from Kingston on a Saturday morning in the cool dawn breeze to wait for the fishermen coming in with their wonderful catches of snapper, goatfish, parrot fish, kingfish, and sprats. We watched the sun come up and laughed and chatted with the others who were waiting for the fishermen.

Finally, there came the boats! As the fishermen pulled up the nets, we could see the beautiful colors of the fish, so fresh that they were still jumping and flipping in the nets. In the early morning sun, it was always a sight to see—the reds and oranges of the snappers, the brilliant blue of the parrot fish. And then there were the conversations to hear!

MR. FISHERMAN: Lawd, what a way de fish dem pretty today.

BUYER: Give me two of those pretty snappers.

MR. FISHERMAN: Which ones?

BUYER: How do you mean which ones?! See those two jumping there?
(Mind you, practically the entire catch was still jumping!)
I want to jerk them for lunch today. Also give me three parrot fish—none with too many bones!

MR. FISHERMAN: You ever hear my parrot fish have bones yet??
(The parrot fish is a beautiful brilliant blue and delicious, but as bony a fish as you will ever find.)

And so it went. We would have a wonderful morning and be back home before nine.

Those who were not able to go directly to the boats could buy from fish vendors who bought them from the fishermen and then peddled to the households. What ingenious carts they developed! Their pushcarts were made of wood, maybe five feet by three feet, with a steering wheel salvaged from an old car and mounted at the back. The steering wheel was usually connected to the front wheels with a bike chain and some rope. The front wheels were made from metal bearings and were covered with strips of old car tires (with treads, where possible!). With a horizontal bar across his lower back, the fish man was able to push a step with his right foot and ride with his left and then push with his left and ride with his right. It was a jump-on, jump-off motion, just as you see children here maneuvering on a scooter. Mind you, these carts were very heavy by the time they were loaded with alternating layers of ice, burlap bags, and fish!

Every fish man had an old set of three-cornered scales that he held high with his hand to give some semblance of weighing the fish. I don't know how accurate this system was, but we all abided happily by it.

Farther out in the country, the fish man rode a bicycle with a big box attached to the back. Because he had a longer way to go, his fish was packed in dry ice. The country children loved to beg and beg for the tiniest sliver of his dry ice, which they would promptly rub on their skin for the tingling, burning sensation!

Because we had very small refrigerators, which were also subject to power shortages, the ice factory was very important. People would buy fifty or one hundred pounds of ice at a time from the factories. What a sight it was to see the huge muscles of the ice factory men as they clumped about in their big rubber boots and wielded their enormous ice tongs. When possible, we went to the ice factory in the early morning because, of course, we hated to see the ice melt so quickly in the hot Jamaican sun. But when the power went out, we all ran to the ice factory with our sheets of zinc to put over the ice for at least a little protection from the heat. Then we hurried home to chill what food we could until the power came back on.

In this chapter, you will find many different types of fish prepared in many different ways. The classic jerked fish found in the jerk huts is coated with jerk paste and then smoked slowly on the grill along with the chicken. But you can use jerk flavors to enhance all sorts of fish dishes, including those baked in the oven or steamed on top of the stove. We also make escovitch fish, which is often served for Lent, and which is also found on every buffet table in Jamaica.

Since some of the tastiest jerk recipes require cooking fish on a grill, let me first recommend that you first buy a grill basket. There are many sizes and shapes of these baskets—some simple rectangles, some elaborately fish-shaped. I prefer the simple rectangular basket, since it will hold the widest variety of cuts and types of fish and shellfish. Using a basket will truly simplify your grilling of fish. No more fish slipping around on the grill when you are trying to turn it! Do be sure, however, to oil the basket thoroughly. You don't want the fish sticking to either the basket or the grill.

The most important consideration in cooking fish of any type is selecting fish that is fresh. You may not be able to buy your fish directly off the boat, but learn to look for signs of freshness wherever you shop. Always check their eyes, yes, their eyes.

When buying whole fish, the eyes should be crystal clear and bright. The gills should still show a little red underneath. The skin should be fresh and shiny. The flesh should be firm, and elastic enough to spring back when pressed with your finger. There should be no smell other than a slight seaweed odor.

When buying steaks and fillets, look for flesh that is firm and moist to the touch. The color should be translucent. If you notice a slimy film on the fish, it is too old.

Grilled fish cooks quickly. A whole fish will cook in 8 to 10 minutes per side over a low fire (225° to 300°F), and fillets will cook in 4 to 5 minutes per side. Since you don't want to char the fish, be sure you use a low fire, with the coals burned down to a heavy layer of gray ash. Because fish easily falls apart, even in a basket, I turn my fish only once during cooking—even if it is *jerked* fish.

This is not the time to leave the grill—fish cooks very quickly and tastes much better when it is light and tender. Remember too that the fish will continue to cook a little after you remove it from the grill.

If you should happen to be in Jamaica, I recommend you try the jerked fish at Miss Emma's jerk stand. The stand is located on a secluded, unpaved road used by locals to get from Kingston to Ocho Rios. This road will shake your insides when you travel on it! But, it's worth it all to find Miss Emma's.

From the looks of it, Miss Emma's is the usual jerk pit with the requisite few tables and chairs, as well as the usual rum, reggae music, sunshine, domino games, and laughter. Miss Emma is a large lady, not in the sense of being fat but in the sense of having an imposing presence. Her age is hard to reckon—anywhere from forty to sixty-five—but she has not lost any of her sex appeal. Miss Emma's welcoming smile will make you feel good just to be there.

The people who come to Miss Emma's enjoy their jerk with a liberal helping of politics when Miss Emma holds court, discussing the latest moves of the government. Truly, one goes to Miss Emma's for the whole experience, not just the food.

When Miss Emma jerks fish she uses a converted oil drum rather than a pit. In this way, she can build a slightly hotter fire than you will use at your home, but Miss Emma is cooking many more fish than you! Her fish are cooked, whole, on aluminum foil to keep them from sticking, since we do not have grill baskets in Jamaica. It takes a little longer to cook a whole fish than fillets, but I prefer it this way, because it keeps the flesh of the fish more intact and moist. The recipe on page 65 comes as close as possible to replicating Miss Emma's jerked fish. You must add the sunshine and music.

Saltfish sit down pon di counter a wait fi bread and butter.

MISS EMMA'S JERK FISH
Serves 4

1 tablespoon Jerk Rub (page 7)
1 whole red snapper (3 to 4
   pounds), cleaned, head and
   tail left on

While some Americans are a little squeamish about seeing a fish cooked with its head on, this method of cooking helps to retain the natural moisture of the fish.

This is delicious served with baked sweet potatoes. Or do like Miss Emma, and serve it with bammy (see page 112) or Festival (page 114) and share your meal with lots of friends and drink plenty of Red Stripe beer.

Prepare a medium fire in a charcoal grill or preheat a gas grill to 350°F. Massage the jerk rub into the fish and let stand for a few minutes. Grill for 8 to 10 minutes on each side, or until opaque throughout. Be careful not to overcook. Place the hot fish on a platter and allow your guests to serve themselves.

INDEPENDENCE DAY GRILLED RED SNAPPER
Serves 8 to 10

1 cup Dry Jerk Seasoning (page 7)
2 cups dry white wine
2 tablespoons vegetable oil
2 whole red snappers (3 to
    4 pounds each), cleaned,
    heads and tails left on

On August 6, 1962, Jamaica became independent from Great Britain, and Independence Day is a very special day to all Jamaicans.

The month leading up to August 6 is always buzzing with activity. We have floats and parades, and the children in school are encouraged to create works of art and write poetry in honor of our independence. There are music competitions and, of course, culinary competitions.

To celebrate Independence Day, I always stage a barbecue in Kingston, where I grew up, in my backyard under the almond tree and Bombay mango tree. These trees are as old as our Independence Day itself and have been the backdrop for many luncheons and picnics. This holiday is a time of family and close friends coming together. Children frolic on the grass, teenagers play games and flirt, and the adults reminisce.

The menu is extensive and always includes this grilled snapper. Serve this with Rice and Peas (page 120) and a green salad.

Mix together the dry jerk seasoning, white wine, and oil. Place the fish in a baking dish and pour the jerk mixture over the fish. Refrigerate for a least 1 hour or up to 2 hours.

Prepare a medium fire in a charcoal grill. Or preheat a gas grill to 350°F. Oil a large grill basket or the grill grids. Place the fish in the basket or on the grill and cook for 8 to 10 minutes on each side, or until opaque throughout. If both fish do not fit in one basket, you may need to cook them in two baskets, or cook one first and then the other. Place the whole fish on a platter and allow your guests to serve themselves.

JERK ASIAN GRILLED RED SNAPPER

Serves 4 to 6

4 scallions, including pale
　　green parts, sliced thinly
3 cloves garlic, diced
3 tablespoons Jerk Rub (page 7)
Grated zest of 2 lemons
2 whole red snappers (about
　　2 pounds each), cleaned,
　　heads and tails left on
¼ cup fresh lemon juice
2 tablespoons soy sauce
2 tablespoons olive oil

Almost any grilled fish recipe can be adapted to jerk cooking, even those with distinctive seasonings of their own. This dish started as my favorite recipe for grilled red snapper, which is seasoned with garlic, ginger, and soy sauce. I replaced the ginger with jerk rub, and voilà! Jerked Asian grilled red snapper. You can do the same with your favorite recipes.

Incidentally, a lot of Jamaican cooking borrows from Asia for the simple reason that in our melting pot of cultures, many people of Asian descent have settled here. Serve this dish with steamed rice.

Prepare a medium fire in a charcoal grill or preheat a gas grill to 350°F.

In a small bowl, combine the scallions, half of the garlic, 2 tablespoons of the jerk rub, and the lemon zest. Stir to blend. Spread half of this mixture inside each of the snappers. In the same bowl, combine the remaining garlic, the remaining 1 tablespoon jerk rub, the lemon juice, soy sauce, and olive oil. Stir to blend and set aside to use for basting the fish.

Oil a grill basket or the grill grids. Place the fish in the basket or on the grill grate. Grill the fish for 8 to 10 minutes on each side, or until opaque throughout, basting with the lemon juice mixture several times during cooking. Serve hot.

CARIBBEAN SALMON STEAKS

Serves 4

8 teaspoons vegetable oil
4 salmon steaks, each about
  2 inches thick
Dry Jerk Seasoning (page 7)
  to taste
Honey-Ginger Dipping Sauce
  (page 127) for serving

These steaks are thicker than most salmon steaks—ask your fishmonger to cut them specially for you. They are delicious with corn on the cob and Jamaican Cole Slaw (page 123). You can substitute kingfish steaks for the salmon.

Prepare a medium fire in a charcoal grill or preheat a gas grill to 350°F.

Rub 2 teaspoons oil over each salmon steak. Sprinkle the dry jerk seasoning over the salmon steaks. Oil a grill basket or the grill grids. Place the fish in the basket or on the grill grate and cook for 5 to 6 minutes on each side, or until still slightly translucent in the center. When the fish flakes just slightly, it is done. Remember that it will continue to cook after you take it off the grill. Serve hot with the dipping sauce.

JERK LOBSTER WITH BUTTER SAUCE
Serves 4

4 rock lobster tails (7 to
    8 ounces each)
½ cup (1 stick) unsalted
    butter, melted
1 teaspoon Jerk Rub (page 7)

BUTTER SAUCE
½ cup (1 stick) unsalted butter
1 scallion, including green tops,
    thinly sliced
2 teaspoons fresh lime juice,
    or to taste
2 to 3 drops hot pepper sauce,
    preferably Scotch bonnet
    sauce, or to taste

This spicy butter sauce is wonderful with many different types of seafood. Serve this lobster dish with garlic bread or Baked Breadfruit (page 115).

Prepare a medium fire in a charcoal grill or preheat a gas grill to 350°F.

To prepare the lobster tails: Cut off the white membrane with kitchen shears and discard. Brush each tail with melted butter and sprinkle with about ¼ teaspoon jerk rub.

To make the butter sauce: In a small saucepan, melt the butter over medium heat. Add the scallion and sauté until just golden, being careful not to let the butter brown or burn. Stir in the lime juice and hot pepper sauce. Set aside.

Oil the grill grids and place the lobster on the grill, meat side down. Cook for 2 to 3 minutes. Turn the lobster over and cook for 7 to 9 minutes, or until opaque throughout. Cooking the lobster with shell side down helps preserve its natural juices. Don't worry if the shell chars.

Serve immediately, with the butter sauce.

JERK LOBSTER WITH COCONUT

Serves 4

4 rock lobster tails (7 to
    8 ounces each), shelled
    and cleaned
½ cup milk
1 cup cream of coconut
2 tablespoons Dry Jerk
    Seasoning (page 7)
Salt and freshly ground black
    pepper to taste
¼ cup grated Parmesan cheese

The flavor of jerk is delicious combined with coconut. The sweetness of the coconut balances the spiciness of the jerk. You will find this a wonderful variation on lobster Thermidor. It is easily made in the oven. Jamaican Fruit Salad (page 133) and Fried Plantains (page 116) go well with this dish. Serve with rice.

Preheat the oven to 400°F. Cut the lobster meat into chunks.

In a large saucepan, combine the milk, cream of coconut, and dry jerk seasoning. Place over medium heat and cook, stirring frequently. Add the lobster, salt, and pepper. Reduce the heat to low and simmer for 7 to 8 minutes to blend all the flavors. Pour into a buttered 8- by 8-inch baking dish and sprinkle with the grated cheese. Bake for about 15 minutes, or until browned.

JERK SCALLOPS
Serves 4 as an appetizer, 2 to 3 as a main course

BROILED JERK SNAPPER FILLET
Serves 2

Do not leave the stove while you are cooking scallops. It is very easy to turn them from an excellent offering from the sea to a pile of rubber because of overcooking. These scallops are delicious as an appetizer or as a main course. If making this as a main course, serve the scallops on a bed of steamed rice that has been moistened with the delicious cooking liquid.

2 tablespoons unsalted butter
2 tablespoons vegetable oil
1 pound sea scallops
2 tablespoons Dry Jerk Seasoning (page 7)
3 tablespoons dry white wine

In a large sauté pan or skillet, melt the butter with the oil over medium-high heat. Add the scallops and sauté just until they turn opaque and lightly golden, about 2 minutes per side. Add the seasoning and the wine, stir to blend, and quickly remove from the heat. Serve at once.

Since it's cooked in your oven's broiler, this snapper lets you enjoy the flavors of jerk fish even if you don't have so much time. Serve this with Jamaican Cole Slaw (page 123) and some sliced mango. And relax!

1 tablespoon Dry Jerk Seasoning (page 7)
Dash of hot pepper sauce
2 tablespoons vegetable oil
One 10-ounce skin-on snapper fillet

Preheat the broiler. In a small bowl, blend the jerk seasoning, pepper sauce, and oil together. Cover the fillet with the mix, being careful to coat it all over. Place on a broiler pan 4 inches from the heat source. Broil for 2 to 3 minutes on one side, or until the fish flakes when tested with a fork. It is not necessary to turn it as it cooks. Serve at once.

STEAMED FISH

Serves 4

2 to 2½ pounds grouper, parrot
   fish, or red snapper fillets
2 tablespoons soy sauce
2 to 3 teaspoons Dry Jerk
   Seasoning (page 7), or to taste
Fish broth or beer for steaming
   (optional)

In Jamaica, most people don't have the kind of steamers that are now available. In order to steam fish, Jamaicans just use a pot with a little water and a tight-fitting lid. Because of the strong Asian influence in Jamaica, steamed foods are very popular.

Place the fish in a steamer rack, if you have one. Sprinkle the fish with the soy sauce and jerk seasoning. Cook in a covered steamer over simmering water for 5 to 6 minutes, or until the fish flakes readily when touched with a fork.

If you don't have a steamer, add about ½ inch of water, broth, or beer to a large pot and place a shallow bowl on a trivet inside the pot. Bring the liquid to a simmer. Place the fish in the bowl, sprinkle with the soy sauce and seasoning, and cover the pot with a tight-fitting lid. Cook for 5 to 6 minutes, or until the fish flakes readily when touched with a fork. Serve hot.

BAKED MAHI-MAHI
Serves 4

Four 8-ounce mahi-mahi fillets,
  or any other firm fish fillets,
  such as tuna or salmon
2 tablespoons dry white wine or
  dry sherry
¾ cup Jerk Marinade (page 8)
¼-inch cube fresh ginger, crushed
1 onion, thinly sliced

The mahi-mahi is a colorful, feisty game fish that is common in Jamaica. It is also known as dorado or dolphinfish (though it is of course unrelated to the dolphin that is a mammal). Its flesh is firm and slightly fatty, and very flavorful.

Cut the fillets into bite-sized pieces. Mix the wine with ½ cup of the Jerk Marinade and the ginger; pour over the fillets. Let stand at room temperature for about 20 minutes.

Preheat the oven to 400°F. Lightly oil a large sheet of aluminum foil or parchment paper. Place the fish and the remaining ¼ cup of the marinade on the foil or paper. Arrange the onion over the fish. Seal the package and bake for 8 to 10 minutes. Remove from the foil or paper. Serve hot.

ESCOVITCH FISH
Serves 4

2 pounds kingfish, mahi-mahi, or
    other firm fish fillets or steaks
Juice of 2 limes
Dry Jerk Seasoning (page 7)
    to taste
Vegetable oil for frying

PICKLING MIXTURE
1 or 2 cucumbers or chochos
    (chayote squash), halved,
    seeded, and cut into long strips
2 onions, thinly sliced
1 tablespoon Jamaican allspice
    berries
1 cup apple cider vinegar
2 tablespoons hot pepper sauce,
    preferably Scotch bonnet
Salt to taste

Escovitch is a popular method for preparing fish in Jamaica. It is very similar to the Spanish escabeche: fish is lightly fried or poached, then pickled for at least 24 hours with a vinegary marinade, and served cold.

Rub the fish with the lime juice and set aside to dry. Sprinkle with dry jerk seasoning on both sides.

In a large, heavy skillet or sauté pan, heat 1 inch of oil over medium-high heat until smoking. Place the fish in the hot oil in a single layer—do not overlap. Reduce the heat to medium and fry until the fish is browned on the bottom, about 2 minutes. Turn and brown on the other side for 2 minutes, or until opaque throughout. Using a slotted metal spatula, transfer to a large nonreactive baking pan, and set aside.

To make the pickling mixture: In a medium saucepan, combine the cucumbers or chochos, onions, pimento berries, vinegar, and pepper sauce and bring to a boil. Add salt. Simmer for 2 minutes, then remove from the heat. Pour the hot pickling mixture over the fish. Let cool, cover, and refrigerate for at least 1 day and up to 3 days. Serve cold.

FRIED SNAPPER WITH ONIONS

Serves 4

2 to 3 tablespoons Jerk Rub
(page 7)
4 small whole snappers (12 to 16
ounces each), cleaned, heads
and tails left on
Vegetable oil for frying
2 small onions, thinly sliced,
rings separated

This combination of jerk spices and fried onions complements the snapper without overwhelming its flavor.

Massage the jerk rub into the fish. In a large, heavy skillet, heat ½ inch of oil over medium-high heat. Add the fish and fry for 2 to 3 minutes, or until golden brown on the bottom. (If all four fish do not fit in your skillet, fry them in batches.) Turn the fish and cook on the second side until golden brown, 2 to 3 minutes. Using a slotted metal spatula, transfer the fish to a plate lined with paper towels and place in a low (150°F) oven to keep warm while you cook the remaining fish and the onions. When the fish are all cooked, fry the onion rings in the hot oil for 2 to 3 minutes, until they are crisp-tender. Drain the onions on paper towels, place the fish on a serving platter, spoon the onions over the fish, and serve immediately.

GRILLED SHRIMP

Serves 4 to 6

2 pounds large shrimp (16 to 20 per pound), shelled and deveined

Vegetable oil for coating

Dry Jerk Seasoning (page 7) to taste

Shrimp cooked on the grill are delicious—you may want to cook a few extra for Shrimp Salad with Fresh Papaya (page 82). Serve these with Baked Plantains (page 116) and an avocado salad. The shrimp can be grilled on skewers or in a grill basket. If you use wooden skewers, be sure to soak them in water for 30 minutes before using them to keep them from catching on fire.

Prepare a medium fire in a charcoal grill, or preheat a gas grill to 350°F.

Coat the shrimp with oil, then sprinkle with dry jerk seasoning. Drain the skewers, if using, and oil the grill grids. Thread the shrimp on the skewers through the tail end and head end to keep them flat. Or, oil a grill basket. Place the skewers on the grill or put the shrimp in the grill basket. Cook for about 2 minutes on each side, or until evenly pink. Do not overcook. Serve hot.

ISLAND SHRIMP
Serves 4

1 to 1¼ pounds large shrimp
  (16 to 20 per pound)
1 (12-ounce) bottle Red Stripe
  beer, or other lager-style beer
¼ cup Key West Key lime juice,
  or substitute ¼ cup freshly
  squeezed lime juice mixed with
  2 teaspoons sugar
2 teaspoons Dry Jerk Seasoning
  (page 7)
¾ cup Honey-Ginger Dipping
  Sauce (page 127)

For true Jamaican flavor, use the specific brands of Key lime juice and beer in this recipe; for not-quite-authentic but delicious results, use the substitutes given at left.

This recipe was developed by Kitchenique, a gourmet shop in Destin, Florida.

Prepare a medium fire in a charcoal grill or preheat the broiler. Rinse the shrimp and devein, leaving the shell on the shrimp. If you do not have a grill basket, soak 8 wooden skewers in water for 30 minutes.

In a medium bowl, combine the beer, lime juice, and dry jerk seasoning. Stir to blend, then add the shrimp and let stand for about 5 minutes. Thread 3 shrimp on each skewer, if using, piercing each through both ends so the shrimp will lie flat. Or, oil a grill basket. Place the skewers on an oiled grill or put the shrimp in the grill basket and grill for 2½ minutes on each side, or until evenly pink. Serve hot, with the dipping sauce.

JERK SHRIMP SALAD

Serves 4

14 ounces medium shrimp
(31 to 35 per pound), shelled
and deveined
2 teaspoons Dry Jerk Seasoning
(page 7) or Walkerswood Jerk
Seasoning
1 tablespoon canola oil
Juice of 1 lime
¼ cup finely chopped red onion
1 large tomato, seeded and
finely chopped
¼ cup finely chopped celery or
green bell pepper
2 teaspoons white wine vinegar
2 tablespoons olive oil
Salt to taste
4 large lettuce leaves
1 large avocado, peeled, pitted,
and thinly sliced
Minced fresh flat-leaf parsley
for garnish

This spicy minced salad was inspired by the conch salad popular in Bermuda. The avocado smooths out the tang of the lime juice.

In a medium bowl, combine the shrimp and jerk seasoning. Let stand at room temperature for 30 minutes.

In a large skillet or sauté pan, heat the canola oil over medium-high heat and stir-fry the shrimp just until it turns pink, about 3 minutes. Transfer the shrimp to a bowl and squeeze the lime juice over it. Let cool, then chop it finely. Return to the bowl and add the onion, tomato, and celery or bell pepper.

In a small bowl, whisk the vinegar and olive oil together. Toss with the shrimp, vegetables, and salt. Cover and refrigerate for at least 30 minutes or up to 1 hour.

To serve, place a lettuce leaf on each of 4 serving plates. Top with slices of avocado and the shrimp mixture, then garnish with parsley.

SHRIMP SALAD WITH FRESH PAPAYA

Serves 2 to 3

8 ounces shrimp, shelled and
   deveined
1 chocho (chayote squash), peeled
½ cup diced celery
¼ small fresh papaya, peeled,
   seeded, and diced
¼ cup mayonnaise
2 teaspoons Dry Jerk Seasoning
   (page 7)
2 tablespoons Passion Fruit
   Sauce (page 152)

The chocho featured in this recipe is known by different names in different areas and by different ethnic groups: chayote squash, christophene, mirliton, and vegetable pear. The chocho is a favorite Jamaican vegetable to use in soups and serve stuffed as a main course.

The mildness of the chocho allows the shrimp to be the star of this dish. If you can't find a chocho, substitute a cucumber, peeled, seeded, and diced. Do not cook the cucumber before adding it to the salad. I like to serve this salad in a pineapple shell. It is very festive and tropical looking.

In a medium saucepan over medium-high heat, bring 2 inches of water to a boil and cook the shrimp until just pink, 1 to 2 minutes. Remove them from the water with a slotted spoon and set aside. Return the water to a boil and add the chocho. Cook until just slightly crunchy, 4 to 5 minutes. Remove the chocho from the water and set aside until cool enough to handle. Slice the chocho in half, then remove the seed and the stringy pith in the middle. Cut into ½-inch dice. Cut the cooked shrimp into ½-inch dice.

In a large bowl, combine the chocho, shrimp, celery, and papaya. Add the mayonnaise, jerk seasoning, and passion fruit sauce. Stir to coat the shrimp, vegetables, and papaya thoroughly. Cover and refrigerate until chilled, and serve cold.

CODFISH AND ACKEE

Serves 6

1 pound salt cod, boned if possible
6 bacon strips
1 tablespoon vegetable oil
1 Scotch bonnet chili, seeded
    and thinly sliced
2 scallions, including pale
    green parts, chopped
1 tomato, diced
1 onion, chopped
One 19-ounce can ackees
Salt and freshly ground
    pepper to taste
1 green bell pepper, seeded,
    deribbed, and cut into
    strips, for garnish

Ackees are fruits with bright red skins and creamy white flesh, brought to Jamaica from West Africa by Captain Bligh in the late 1700s. But you will not be able to get fresh ackees unless you go to the islands, as there are import restrictions on this fruit (eating unripe ackee causes a bad stomachache!). But no cookbook that deals with Jamaica would be complete without a recipe for codfish and ackee, which is considered to be our national dish. Canned ackees are available in Latino and West Indian stores.

In a large pot, cover the salt cod with cold water and soak for 30 to 40 minutes. This will help to remove the excess salt from the fish. Pour out the original water and add 4 cups cold water. Bring to a full boil, then drain. Remove any bones and skin and flake the codfish.

In a large skillet, fry the bacon until crisp. Transfer to paper towels to drain. Crumble and set aside.

In a separate pan, heat the oil over medium heat. Add the chili, scallions, tomato, and onion. Sauté until the onion is translucent, 3 to 4 minutes.

Drain the ackees and stir into the pan along with the codfish. Season with salt and pepper. Reduce the heat to low, cover, and cook for about 5 minutes, or until all the flavors are blended. Using a slotted metal spatula, transfer the fish, ackees, and vegetables to plates. Garnish each serving with the crumbled bacon and pepper strips.

FISH TEA

Serves 8 to 10

8 cups cold water

2 pounds fish heads or fish
carcasses, from parrot fish,
snapper, kingfish, or mahi-mahi

3 or 4 potatoes, peeled and cubed

1 tomato, chopped

1 branch (2 to 3 inches long)
fresh thyme, or 1 teaspoon
dried thyme

½ onion, diced

1 whole Scotch bonnet chili

Salt and freshly ground pepper
to taste

This wonderful light soup is almost the equivalent of America's chicken soup as far as its perceived medicinal qualities. It is frequently made with parrot fish, which has a delicious flavor but many, many little bones. Fish tea is usually served in big mugs or cups, not in dainty little soup bowls.

In a soup pot, combine the water and fish and bring to a boil. Reduce the heat to medium, cover, and simmer for 30 minutes. Strain and reserve both the broth and the fish.

Remove all the flesh from the bones, then discard the bones. Return the fish to the broth, along with the remaining ingredients. Bring to a boil again, then reduce the heat to a simmer. Cook, uncovered, until the potatoes are tender, about 20 minutes, adding more water if necessary. Remove the chili without breaking it in order to get the flavor and not the heat. Serve very hot in large mugs or deep soup bowls.

CHAPTER 5

BEEF, LAMB, AND GOAT

In Jamaica, we never had access to the better cuts of beef until twenty to thirty years ago. At that time, the American bauxite companies came to the island and developed what became our largest industry. For many years, Jamaica was the world's largest supplier of bauxite, an ore used in the production of aluminum. Eventually, the bauxite companies developed cattle ranches on the plains of the island to satisfy their American workers' desire for beef. Until then, cattle raising had been a very casual affair, just a few cows here and there, and without the goal of producing tender cuts. Consequently, Jamaicans cooked only beef dishes such as stews, where tougher cuts of meat were tenderized by long, slow, moist cooking. Since then, however, we have discovered the joys of grilled steaks flavored with jerk seasoning and rare roasts smeared with jerk paste.

Other meats that we have long enjoyed include kid and goat. It is wonderful to see all the little kid goats (called *cabritos* by Spanish speakers) scampering up the mountains in Jamaica—you see them everywhere! Like pigs and chickens, goats are easily grown, take up little room, and eat a variety of foods. An additional bonus is that goat meat is lean, and one goat is enough to feed 12 to 15 people. If you can find a source for goat, you can make curry goat yourself!

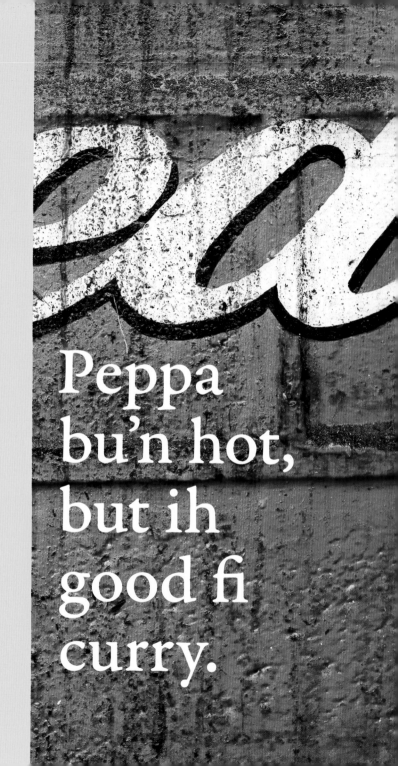

Peppa bu'n hot, but ih good fi curry.

JAMAICAN BEEF KABOBS

Serves 6

3 cups Jerk Marinade (page 8)
2 teaspoons olive oil
2-pound beef sirloin, cut into
   2-inch cubes
18 pearl onions, peeled
2 zucchini, cut into chunks
18 mushrooms, stems removed
18 cherry tomatoes

These kabobs are wonderful served with a pilaf or steamed rice. I prefer to cook the vegetables on separate skewers, since they take less time than the beef and can turn to mush if they are overcooked. Serve this with steamed rice or flat bread.

In a resealable plastic bag, combine 2 cups of the marinade and olive oil. Add the meat and rotate the bag thoroughly coat the meat. Refrigerate for at least 4 hours or as long as overnight, turning the bag occasionally.

Prepare a medium fire in a charcoal grill or preheat a gas grill to 350°F. Soak 12 wooden skewers in water for 30 minutes.

Remove the meat from the bag and skewer it alternately with the onions. Place the zucchini, mushrooms, and cherry tomatoes on separate skewers. Place the skewers on the grill and grill the meat, basting frequently with the remaining 1 cup marinade, for a total of 10 to 12 minutes, turning the skewers frequently to brown the meat evenly. Grill the vegetables for a total of 6 to 8 minutes, basting frequently with the marinade and turning frequently. Serve hot.

CARIBBEAN BEEF FILET

Serves 4

½ cup mayonnaise

6 tablespoons Dry Jerk Seasoning (page 7)

1 teaspoon hot pepper sauce

2 pounds beef tenderloin

Corn, safflower, or olive oil for coating, plus 1 tablespoon for cooking

This delicious "blackened" filet will make your mouth water. It combines the Cajun blackened cooking technique and the wonderful flavors of the tropics. A whole beef filet is about 5 or 6 pounds; ask your butcher to cut you a 2-pound piece for this recipe. Thinly sliced, the beef makes a delicious appetizer.

Preheat the oven to 325°F.

In a small bowl, stir together the mayonnaise, 1 tablespoon of the jerk seasoning, and the hot pepper sauce. Set aside.

Coat the filet lightly with oil. Put the remaining 5 tablespoons of the jerk seasoning and the oiled beef in a heavy, resealable plastic bag, close the bag, and massage the seasoning into the meat. The oil will help hold the seasoning on.

Pour the 1 tablespoon oil into a large oven-proof skillet. Place over high heat and heat until almost smoking; the surface of the oil will shimmer. Add the filet and sear the meat on all sides. Transfer the pan to the oven and roast for 15 minutes, or until an instant-read thermometer inserted in the center of the meat registers 140° to 145°F for rare. Allow the meat to rest for about 5 minutes, then slice and serve with the spicy mayonnaise.

STIR-FRIED BEEF

Serves 4 to 6

One 1-pound boneless
   round steak
1 tablespoon cornstarch
1½ teaspoons sugar
½ cup water
⅓ cup soy sauce
1 tablespoon dry sherry or
   Chinese Shaoxing wine
2 tablespoons vegetable oil
¼ pound snow peas, ends
   trimmed and strings removed
1 carrot, peeled and sliced
   diagonally
1 large onion, coarsely chopped
1 small zucchini, diagonally sliced
1 tablespoon Dry Jerk Seasoning
   (page 7), or to taste
Steamed rice for serving

Jerk seasoning adds a delightful dash to this Asian-style dish.

Place the steak in the freezer for about 15 minutes, or until partially frozen. Slice across the grain into strips about 3 inches by ¼ inch; set aside. In a small bowl, combine the cornstarch, sugar, water, soy sauce, and sherry or wine; stir to blend, then set aside. Everything must be prepared before you start cooking; stir-fry cooking is very quick!

Heat a wok or a large skillet over medium-high heat. Add the oil and swirl the pan to coat the sides with oil. Heat for 2 minutes, or just until the oil starts to smoke. Add the beef and stir-fry until browned, 2 to 3 minutes. Using a wire skimmer, transfer the beef to a plate.

Add the vegetables to the wok and stir-fry for 3 minutes, or until crisp-tender. Return the beef to the wok. Sprinkle with the dry jerk seasoning and continue to stir-fry for 1 minute. Stir in the soy mixture and stir-fry until the sauce has thickened, about 2 minutes. Serve at once, over rice.

CARIBBEAN BURGERS

Serves 4

1½ pounds lean ground beef, chuck, or turkey

4 teaspoons Dry Jerk Seasoning (page 7)

2 tablespoons catsup

2 tablespoons Honey-Ginger Dipping Sauce (page 127)

2 tablespoons vegetable oil

4 hamburger buns

4 slices Cheddar cheese

4 slices cored fresh pineapple

With jerk seasonings, honey-ginger enhanced catsup, and grilled fresh pineapple, this is truly a cheeseburger that tastes like paradise.

Light a medium fire in a charcoal grill, preheat a gas grill to 350°F, or heat a large skillet over medium-high heat. Season the beef with the dry jerk seasoning and mix well. Form into 4 patties.

In a small bowl, combine the catsup and dipping sauce. Oil the grill grids or heat the oil in the pan over medium-high heat. Add the patties to the grill or the pan and cook until browned, about 3 minutes on each side. If you are using a grill, grill the pineapple slices for about 1 minute per side. Lightly toast the buns.

To serve, place the meat patties on the buns and top each with 1 slice of cheese and 1 slice of pineapple. Dress with the catsup mixture. Serve at once.

BEEF BRISKET À LA HELEN

Serves 8

1 beef brisket (5 to 6 pounds)
¾ cup Jerk Marinade (page 8)

This dish is foolproof for novices and cooks who are very busy with other things. The meat cooks away for hours in a low oven and comes out delicious and very tender.

Place the brisket and marinade in a resealable plastic bag and rotate the bag several times to thoroughly coat the meat. Refrigerate for at least 2 to 3 hours, turning once or twice.

Preheat the oven to 300°F. Place the brisket and marinade in a roasting pan and cover with aluminum foil. Bake for 3½ to 4 hours, or until the internal temperature is 140° to 145°F for rare or 150°F for medium. Let the meat rest for 5 or 10 minutes before carving, and serve with the pan drippings.

ROAST BEEF À LA CALYPSO

Serves 6 to 8

1 cup Jerk Rub (page 7)
1 tablespoon vegetable oil
1 rolled beef rump roast
   (4 to 6 pounds)

My family fights for the leftovers from this dish so we can make a variation on the French dip sandwich. We mix any leftover pan juices with Honey-Ginger Dipping Sauce (page 127) and pour that over the meat.

In a resealable plastic bag, combine the jerk rub and oil. Add the meat and rotate the bag to thoroughly coat the meat. Refrigerate for at least 5 hours or as long as overnight, turning the bag occasionally.

Preheat the oven to 325°F. Place the meat on a rack in a roasting pan and roast for 2 to 2½ hours, or until a meat thermometer reaches 140°F for rare or 150°F for medium-rare. Let the meat stand for about 5 minutes before slicing 1 to 1½ inches thick to serve.

2 tablespoons vegetable oil

One 2-pound boneless chuck
   roast, cut into 1-inch cubes

4 cups water, plus 1½ tablespoons

1 tablespoon packed brown sugar

1½ teaspoons cider vinegar

1 onion, sliced

1 garlic clove, minced

2 tablespoons Jerk Rub
   (page 7)

4 carrots, peeled and cut into
   2-inch chunks

4 potatoes, peeled and cut
   into 2-inch chunks

Salt and freshly ground
   pepper to taste

1½ tablespoons cornstarch

This tasty version of beef stew is mildly flavored with jerk rub. If you plan to freeze this dish, omit the potatoes, as cooked potatoes do not hold up well in the freezer. This stew is delicious cooked on top of the stove or in a slow cooker.

In a large Dutch oven, heat the oil over medium-high heat. Add the meat and brown well on all sides, 8 to 10 minutes. Stir in the 4 cups water, the brown sugar, vinegar, onion, garlic, and jerk rub. Reduce the heat to medium, cover, and bring the liquid to a simmer. Cook for 2 hours.

Add the carrots and potatoes, cover, and cook for another 20 to 30 minutes, or until the vegetables are tender. Add salt and pepper.

In a small bowl, combine the cornstarch and the 1½ tablespoons water and stir until smooth. Gradually stir this mixture into the stew. Cook, uncovered, stirring frequently, until the stew is thickened, 3 to 5 more minutes. Serve hot. This tastes even better on the second day.

VARIATION:

To make the stew in a slow cooker, omit the oil and reduce the water to 3 cups. Place all the ingredients in the pot except for the cornstarch mixture. Cook on high for 20 minutes, then reduce the heat to low. Cook for 6 to 8 hours, or until very tender. About 20 minutes before serving, stir in the cornstarch mixture and cook for 15 to 20 minutes to thicken the gravy.

MEAT LOAF WITH JERK

Serves 6

1½ pounds lean ground beef or
  ground turkey
2 large eggs
1 large onion, finely chopped
1 green bell pepper, seeded,
  deribbed, and finely chopped
1 tablespoon Dry Jerk Seasoning
  (page 7)
One 8-ounce can tomato sauce
1 tablespoon packed brown sugar
1 cup fresh bread crumbs

This is an easy dish to fix in the morning before work; just put it in the refrigerator, then pop it into the oven along with some sweet potatoes when you come home.

Lightly oil a 9-by-5-inch loaf pan. Preheat the oven to 350°F.

In a large bowl, combine all the ingredients and mix until well blended. Put the mixture in the loaf pan and smooth the top. Bake for 1 hour, or until the internal temperature reads 155°F.

Remove from the oven and let stand for about 15 minutes, then pour off the pan drippings. Loosen the meat from the sides of the pan and invert onto a serving platter. Serve hot or cold, cut into slices.

These wonderful meat pies, similar to Mexican empanadas, are one of the most popular Jamaican foods. Along with jerk and bammy, beef patties are essential to the Jamaican way of life.

*Patties are not a special treat; they are eaten every day by the rich and the poor, by children and by old people, like hamburgers are in America. They are eaten in offices, served as lunch, a snack, or dinner. Interestingly, patties are rarely **made** at home. Instead, people stand in line at a patty stand waiting for one that is fresh and hot. Depending on the popularity of the patty shop at the moment, the line can reach all the way around the building! We visit with one another while waiting our turn for the little pies, or we become friends with those we don't already know.*

There are patty shops of renown, such as Tastees. When I was a little girl, it was Bruce's, and then there is Angel Flake. You see, we regularly fall in love with one particular patty from one particular vendor, and it is like a love affair. We must have that patty, and only that patty, but if the recipe changes in the slightest, we fall out of love. There is very little that the patty shop owner can do to entice us back. We immediately search for a new patty shop, and soon everyone is hearing praises about it, and we have totally forgotten our previous allegiance.

Why are patties so good? The crust, the crust, the crust! Patties are usually made with a beef filling, but there are also seafood patties. Patties can be mild or hot, and usually the vendor will ask which you prefer.

Then there are cocktail patties: little bites that are served as appetizers. The patty purist will tell you that a patty can be eaten only freshly baked, but I find that they can be frozen and then rebaked very successfully.

PASTRY

4 cups all-purpose flour
½ teaspoon baking powder
1 teaspoon ground turmeric
1 teaspoon salt
1 cup vegetable shortening or lard, at room temperature (look for nonhydrogenated shortening)
About 1 cup very cold water

FILLING

2 onions
3 scallions, including green tops
2 Scotch bonnet chilies
1½ pounds ground beef or chuck
2 tablespoons vegetable oil
1½ cups fine bread crumbs
¾ teaspoon ground thyme
¾ teaspoon ground turmeric
Salt and freshly ground pepper to taste
1 cup water

To make the pastry: In a large bowl, combine the flour, baking powder, turmeric, and salt. Stir with a whisk to blend. Cut in the shortening with a pastry blender or 2 dinner knives until the dough has the consistency of cornmeal. Gradually add just enough cold water to hold the dough together, mixing it in with a fork. Take care not to overwork your dough; it should just come together. Form the dough into a disk and wrap it in plastic wrap. Refrigerate the dough while you make the filling, or for as long as overnight. If chilled overnight, remove from the refrigerator 15 minutes before rolling out.

To make the filling: Mince the onions, scallions, and chilies. Add to the beef and mix well. In a Dutch oven or large skillet, heat the oil over medium heat, then cook the meat mixture, stirring frequently, until lightly browned, about 10 minutes. Stir in the bread crumbs, seasonings, and water. Cover and simmer for 20 to 30 minutes, or until thickened; the mixture should be just wet, not runny or dry. Remove from the heat and let cool while you roll out the dough.

Preheat the oven to 400°F. Divide the dough into 24 even-sized pieces. On a lightly floured surface, roll out each piece of dough to a thickness of about ⅜ inch—a little thicker than pie dough—and cut into a round using a can, glass, or cup (about 4 inches across). Place the rounds on ungreased baking sheets. Cover the rounds you are not working on with a damp cloth. Spoon filling onto a round to cover half of the pastry, leaving a ¼-inch border. Fold the other half over and seal the edges by crimping with a fork. Bake the patties for 30 to 35 minutes, or until golden. Serve hot.

JAMAICAN JERK MEATBALLS
Serves 4

¼ cup packed brown sugar
1 tablespoon apple cider vinegar
1½ cups catsup
1 cup water
1 pound ground beef
1 small onion, finely chopped
1 teaspoon minced garlic
1 teaspoon Dry Jerk Seasoning
  (page 7)
1 egg, lightly beaten
½ cup milk
¼ cup dried bread crumbs
¼ cup vegetable oil

In Jamaica, we love meatballs. This recipe is my way of combining meatballs with the even more popular jerk. Serve these as a main dish with Jerk Sweet Potato Oven Fries (page 117) on the side, or they make wonderful submarine sandwiches with some Caribbean-style pepper sauce and grated cheddar cheese.

Preheat the oven to 350°F. In a small bowl, stir the sugar, vinegar, catsup, and water together. Set aside. In a separate bowl, combine the beef, onion, garlic, jerk seasoning, egg, milk, and bread crumbs and mix well with your hands until blended. Form the beef mixture into 8 balls, each about 1½ to 2 inches.

In a large skillet or sauté pan, heat the oil over medium-high heat. Fry the meatballs in the oil until browned on all sides, about 4 minutes. Using a slotted spoon, transfer the meatballs to a casserole dish. Pour the sauce over the meatballs and bake, uncovered, for about 45 minutes, or until the liquid is nearly gone. Serve hot.

LAMB KABOBS

Serves 6

1½ cups Jerk Marinade (page 8)
1 boneless leg of lamb (2 to
  3 pounds), cut into 1½- to
  2-inch cubes
18 pearl onions, peeled
2 or 3 red, green, and/or
  yellow bell peppers, seeded,
  deribbed, and cut into
  1-inch squares

Although not really a traditional combination, lamb and jerk seasoning are a delicious twosome. Serve this with rice pilaf or Baked Breadfruit (page 115).

In a resealable plastic bag, combine 1 cup of the marinade and the lamb cubes. Rotate the bag to coat all the meat. Refrigerate for 4 to 6 hours, turning the bag occasionally.

Prepare a medium fire in a charcoal grill or preheat a gas grill to 350°F. Soak 12 wooden skewers in water 30 minutes; drain. Alternately thread the meat, onions, and peppers on the skewers. Place the skewers in the marinade until you are ready to grill.

Drain the skewers well and grill, basting occasionally with the remaining ½ cup marinade and turning frequently, until browned on all sides, for a total of 8 to 10 minutes for medium doneness.

LAMB FAJITAS
Serves 4 to 6

One 2-pound boneless shoulder
   or leg of lamb, butterflied
¾ cup Jerk Marinade (page 8)
1 large onion, sliced
2 green bell peppers, seeded,
   deribbed, and cut into
   large chunks
12 (10-inch) flour tortillas
1 tablespoon vegetable oil
2 teaspoons Dry Jerk
   Seasoning (page 7)
1 lime, halved
Shredded lettuce and salsa
   to serve

This is true melting pot cookery. Mexican fajitas are one of the most popular dishes in the United States these days. This Jamaican version combines the wonderful taste and texture of lamb with the balanced spiciness of jerk seasoning. Get your butcher to butterfly the lamb for you. This is also very tasty when made with flank steak. Serve to friends, along with salsa, Red Stripe beer, and plenty of music!

In a resealable plastic bag, combine the meat, marinade, and vegetables. Rotate the bag to coat the ingredients. Refrigerate for at least 4 hours or up to 6 hours, turning the bag occasionally.

Light a medium fire in a charcoal grill or preheat a gas grill to 350°F. Remove the lamb from the bag and grill for 4 minutes on each side, until browned. Do not overcook—you will complete the cooking with the vegetables in a skillet. Remove the meat from the grill and cut it into thin slices.

Stack the tortillas and wrap them in aluminum foil. Place the package on the grill to warm while you finish the lamb and vegetables. In a skillet or on a griddle, heat the oil over medium-high heat and add the vegetables and dry jerk seasoning. Sauté for about 4 minutes, add the meat and sauté for another 3 minutes, or until the meat is medium-rare and the vegetables are crisp-tender. Squeeze the lime over the mixture. Serve immediately on the warm flour tortillas with shredded lettuce and salsa.

ROASTED LEG OF JERK LAMB

Serves 6 to 8

½ leg of lamb, bone-in (7 to 8 pounds)
4 to 6 cloves garlic
1 tablespoon olive oil
5 tablespoons Dry Jerk Seasoning (page 7)
1 cup beef broth, heated
¼ cup dry red wine
Salt and freshly ground pepper to taste
Honey-Ginger Dipping Sauce (page 127), optional

For this recipe, the herbs that usually season roast lamb are replaced with a jerk blend.

Preheat the oven to 450°F. Cut small slits in the surface of the leg of lamb and stud with the garlic cloves. Rub the outside of the leg of lamb with the oil. Coat evenly with the dry jerk seasoning, massaging as much seasoning into the meat as you can. Place on a rack in a roasting pan.

Roast for 20 minutes; then reduce the temperature to 350°F and continue to roast for about 1 hour, or until an instant-read thermometer inserted in the thickest part of the meat registers 145°F for medium-rare.

Transfer the meat to a platter and allow it to rest for 5 to 10 minutes before slicing. While the meat rests, add the broth and wine to the roasting pan. Bring to a boil over medium heat and cook, stirring to scrape up the browned bits from the bottom of the pan, until the liquid has reduced by about one-third and has a syrupy consistency. Season with salt and pepper. Slice the meat and serve with the pan juices and the Honey-Ginger Dipping Sauce, if using.

LAMB SHANK STEW
Serves 4

3 tablespoons vegetable oil

4 lamb shanks, trimmed of
  excess fat

1 large onion, coarsely chopped

4 large carrots, peeled and
  chopped

1 tablespoon Jerk Rub (page 7)

3 cups water

2 tablespoons tomato paste

One 8-ounce can tomato sauce

Not only are lamb shanks very economical, they are also among the most flavorful of the cuts of lamb. This is a complete meal when cooked with carrots and onions. I also like it with roasted potatoes, although sometimes I add some cubed potatoes along with the liquid ingredients.

In a large Dutch oven over medium-high heat, heat the oil and cook the lamb shanks for 6 to 8 minutes, until browned on all sides. Remove the shanks from the pot and add the onion and carrots to the pan. Sauté the vegetables until they are just soft, about 5 minutes. Add the jerk rub and stir for 30 seconds, then add the lamb shanks, water, tomato paste, and tomato sauce. Bring to a simmer, reduce the heat to low, cover, and cook for 2 hours, until the lamb and vegetables are tender.

VARIATION:

To make in a slow cooker, brown the meat and sauté the vegetables on the stove top as above. Place the meat and vegetables in a slow cooker and sprinkle with the jerk rub. Add 2 cups of water, the tomato paste, and the tomato sauce. Cook on low for 8 hours.

CURRY GOAT

Serves 4

2 pounds goat meat from the
   leg or shoulder
1 large onion, chopped
1 clove garlic, minced
1 habanero or Scotch bonnet
   chili, seeded (or not, depending
   on how hot you want it) and
   chopped
2 tablespoons curry powder
Salt and freshly ground
   pepper to taste
2 tablespoons vegetable oil
2 cups water

Curry goat is one of Jamaica's national dishes. We always serve it for special occasions, and it seems to be one of the best-remembered dishes by tourists. Certainly it is one of the dishes I am frequently asked about by Americans who have traveled to Jamaica. As to where to find goat meat, call around to local specialty butchers and farmers. The meat will have bones, but they will soften during cooking. Serve this over white rice with green bananas, fried plantains, and chutney, or anything you like! You can also add potatoes or tomatoes to the curry as it cooks.

Trim any fat from the goat and then chop the meat into bite-sized pieces with a cleaver. Don't worry about any bones; they will become soft and chewable after cooking. In a resealable plastic bag, combine the meat, onion, garlic, chili, curry powder, salt, and pepper. Rotate to coat the meat and onion. Refrigerate for 1 hour.

In a large Dutch oven, heat the oil over medium heat and add the meat, vegetables, and seasoning. Brown the meat on all sides, about 6 minutes. Add the water, cover, and bring to a simmer. Reduce the heat to low and cook for 1 hour. Taste and adjust the seasoning and add more water if needed. Continue to cook until the meat and bones are tender, 20 to 25 minutes longer.

CHAPTER 6

SIDE DISHES

Jamaicans buy their jerked food from roadside stands: pork is sold by the pound, chicken is sold in quarters, and one says in a *very* loud voice: "Gimme one-fourth of a chicken, please, and half a pound of pork."

These are usually served on pieces of aluminum foil, with the juices dripping. If you are lucky, there will be napkins available. The accompanying question usually is, "Wha' you have wid it? Me have festival, hard dough bread, roasted breadfruit, roasted yam, and sweet potatoes."

Many of these wonderful finger foods can be made at home, so you can enjoy them with your jerked foods.

Festival is a relatively new food. It appeared on the Jamaican culinary scene only a few decades ago, but it is already a must. Eating a piece of festival is like eating a slightly sweet hush puppy without the onions, or a piece of fried corn bread that is much lighter and fluffier in texture.

Hard dough bread is a little like a chewy bagel. It is never baked at home. As for getting a recipe to pass on, it is impossible. The commercial makers tell me they do not have the recipe written down; they know it by heart—and keep it a secret.

Festival is featured at roadside stands on Helshire Beach. This beach is where all Kingstonians congregate, about eleven miles outside of Kingston at the foot of the South Helshire Hills. Laughter rings out there, where Jamaican families of all classes come together. One sees fishermen going out and coming back from the sea, most of them wearing dreadlocks and looking like Rastafarians.

My family goes there mainly for breakfast on a Saturday or a Sunday morning. Breakfast at Helshire consists of fried fish, bammy, and festival, which is cooked fresh in little stands on the beach.

All fried fish in Jamaica is served with bammy, which is a very bland, breadlike product. We eat it more for the texture than the flavor. Bammy is made of cassava, a starchy tuberous root, which is also known as yuca and manioc. It is the same plant that gives us tapioca. There are two types of cassava: sweet and bitter. The sweet cassava is used to make bammy, whereas the bitter cassava makes a wonderful starch, which is used in abundance for all the children's clothes in Jamaica, where even the poorest child goes to school in clothes that are stiffly starched and ironed.

Bammy is like Jamaican beef patties in that it is very rarely made at home. The only recipe I have ever seen is one that came from Norma Benghiat. I have never made bammy myself, nor have my mother or grandmother or any of my aunts. We buy bammy from bammy women. When my father visits me from Jamaica, he brings up bammy, which I keep in the freezer. And if you go to Jamaica, I recommend you do the same, because, you see, making bammy is a lot of work.

To make bammy, you have to peel and very finely grate some sweet cassava. You add about 1 teaspoon salt for every 4 cups grated cassava. Then you press out the excess liquid through a sieve. After that it's simply a matter of making bammy cakes about 6 inches in diameter and frying them for about 5 minutes on each side.

Before eating store-bought or homemade bammy you must soak each one in a shallow bowl filled with 1 cup milk that is mixed with a dash of salt for about 10 minutes. Then fry, grill, or bake them. I prefer to bake them for about 15 minutes in a preheated 350°F oven with a little butter on them.

A dish that must go in all Jamaican cookbooks is our Jamaican rice and peas (called peas and rice in the Bahamas). In Jamaica, we have two versions—one made with red kidney beans, which is served throughout the year, and the other made with fresh gungo (pronounced goongo) peas, served mainly at Christmastime.

These dishes also accompany jerk pork, chicken, or fish, but would be served in a restaurant or in the home, as it would be a little difficult to serve rice and peas in the standard aluminum foil of the jerk shacks!

Other important side dishes in Jamaica are made from plantains, breadfruit, yams, and sweet potatoes. Plantains can be baked or fried, and breadfruit, yams, and sweet potatoes can be roasted in coals in a fire pit or grill, or in the oven. All of them are available from jerk shacks, where they are the perfect foods to serve with jerked meats.

Too much callaloo

mek peppa-pot stew bitter.

FESTIVAL

1 cup all-purpose flour
1 cup cornmeal
2 teaspoons sugar
Pinch of salt
¼ teaspoon ground nutmeg
¼ teaspoon baking soda
½ teaspoon vanilla extract
About ½ cup milk
Vegetable or peanut oil for
   deep-frying

A must with any jerk dish, festival is a sweetened cousin to hush puppies. Allow about two pieces of festival per serving. Serve with jerk pork or fried fish and bammy.

In a large bowl, combine the flour, cornmeal, sugar, salt, nutmeg, and baking soda. Stir with a whisk to blend. Add the vanilla and just enough milk to hold the dry ingredients together in a stiff batter.

Preheat oven to 200°F. In a Dutch oven or deep fryer, heat 3 inches of oil to 370°F.

Pinch off pieces of dough and form into cylinders about 4 inches long and 1½ inches in diameter. Fry a few at a time until golden brown, about 4 minutes, turning once. Be sure that the inside is cooked. Using a wire skimmer, transfer to paper towels to drain. Keep hot in the oven while frying the rest. Serve hot.

BAKED BREADFRUIT

Serves 6

Vegetable oil for coating
1 breadfruit (2 to 3 pounds)

Breadfruit is native to the Pacific and Indian Oceans. It was first collected by William Bligh of the Bounty *to cheaply feed slaves in the British colonies, including Jamaica. It's always served cooked— either baked, grilled, or steamed.*

Preheat the oven to 350°F. Oil the breadfruit and bake for 1½ to 2 hours, or until fragrant and soft when pressed with your finger. Peel and wrap in a damp cloth until you are ready to serve (you can hold it for several hours before serving). Slice thinly and serve.

VARIATION:

The next day, if any breadfruit is left, it is delicious thinly sliced and deep-fried for chips. These are a wonderful accompaniment for cold drinks.

FRIED
PLANTAINS
Serves 4 to 6

Fried plantains accompany almost every meal in Jamaica.

....

2 pounds ripe (black) plantains
¼ cup vegetable oil
1 tablespoon unsalted butter (optional, but it makes the plantain taste even more delicious)

....

Cut each unpeeled plantain lengthwise into 4 thick strips, then peel; or cut into quarters, then peel and cut on the diagonal to make 1-inch rounds. In a large cast-iron skillet, heat the oil over medium-high heat and then add the butter, if using. Add some plantain slices. (Be careful not to add too many slices at once, as this will lower the temperature of the oil.) Fry until golden brown, about 1½ minutes on each side. Using a slotted metal spatula, transfer the pieces to paper towels to drain. Keep hot in a low (200°F) oven while frying the rest. Serve hot.

BAKED
PLANTAINS
Serves 6

Baked plantains are a good alternative when you are trying to avoid fried foods. Use partially ripe plantains for this dish.

....

2 yellow plantains with black flecks

....

Preheat the oven to 350°F. Oil a baking sheet.

Peel the plantains, leaving one strip of skin. Cut the plantains in thirds crosswise. Place them, skin side down, on the baking sheet. Bake for 35 to 40 minutes, or until soft. Cool, completely peel the skin, and slice the plantains lengthwise. Serve warm or at room temperature.

116

BAKED
SWEET POTATOES
Serves 4

JERK SWEET POTATO
OVEN FRIES
Serves 4

In the jerk shacks, sweet potatoes are just put on the coals and baked for about an hour. The aroma of browning potatoes is wonderful as it mingles with the jerk foods. You can also bake them in the oven. Serve these with jerk chicken. You are in for a treat!

You can also use yams or regular potatoes here. I prefer the sweet potato; it is firmer in texture than a yam and has a better flavor with the jerk seasoning than regular potatoes.

4 sweet potatoes
4 teaspoons vegetable oil
Unsalted butter for topping (optional)

1 tablespoon canola oil
1 teaspoon Dry Jerk Seasoning (page 7) or
    Busha Browne's Jerk Seasoning
4 medium sweet potatoes, scrubbed

Preheat the oven to 350°F. Wash the potatoes well and dry. Rub the skin of each potato with 1 teaspoon of the oil. Bake for 1 hour, or until soft when pierced with a knife. Split each sweet potato down the middle and top with butter, if you like.

Preheat the oven to 375°F. In a small bowl, stir the oil and jerk seasoning together. Set aside. Cut the potatoes into lengthwise wedges about ¾-inch thick. Place them in a baking dish large enough to hold them in a single layer, pour the oil mixture over, and toss to coat. Bake, uncovered, until fork-tender, about 30 minutes.

JAMMIN' ROAST POTATOES

Serves 4 to 6

3 pounds potatoes
1 medium red onion, cut into
¼-inch slices
1 medium yellow onion, cut
into ¼-inch slices
1 red bell pepper, seeded,
deribbed, and cut into
¼-inch pieces
5 cloves garlic, minced
1 habanero or serrano chili,
seeded and minced
5 tablespoons vegetable oil
3 tablespoons Dry Jerk
Seasoning (page 7)
2 tablespoons hot sauce
1 teaspoon freshly ground
black pepper
1 teaspoon salt

These spicy potatoes will "catch a fire" anytime they are served—breakfast, lunch, or dinner. You can always raise the heat by adding more chili pepper, but remember that it is easier to raise the heat of this dish than to lower it, so taste them along the way, and serve them with hot pepper sauce in case your guests want to spice it up.

Scrub the potatoes and dice into ½-inch cubes. Place the diced potatoes in a bowl and cover with cold water, and let them soak for about 20 minutes. Drain the potatoes and spread them out on a towel to let them dry a bit.

Preheat the oven to 350°F. Place the potatoes in a bowl with the onions, bell pepper, garlic, and chili, and toss them with the vegetable oil to coat. Mix the dry jerk seasoning, hot sauce, black pepper, and salt with the potatoes, tossing them to evenly coat the potatoes. Pour the potato mixture onto a baking sheet and spread out evenly. Put in the oven and, after 20 minutes, turn the vegetables. Continue baking for another 20 minutes, or until the potatoes are lightly browned and crisp (if they aren't, continue baking and check them every 10 minutes). Remove from the oven, scrape into a serving bowl, and serve hot.

RICE AND PEAS
Serves 6

1½ cups dried red kidney beans,
    picked over, rinsed, and
    soaked overnight
1 clove garlic, crushed
4 cups water
Salt to taste
2 slices bacon, chopped
2 cups coconut milk
Freshly ground pepper to taste
1 scallion, including green
    parts, chopped
1 sprig fresh thyme
1 whole Scotch bonnet chili
2 cups long-grain white rice

Jamaican rice and peas is a staple of our diet, and we use coconut milk in it to give it a characteristically sweet flavor. Rice and peas can be cooked seven days a week. My cousins, Michael and Richard, now grown men, were voracious eaters as teenagers. For their Sunday evening supper, they were known to make a rice and peas and plantain sandwich that consisted of an entire loaf of sliced bread—yes, about twenty slices—and in between each slice was packed rice and peas, gravy, and fried plantains. Both boys grew to be well over six feet tall, and one is now a professor of English at the University of Massachusetts. But pity my poor Aunt Vie, who always thought she had made enough food to last for two more days with her Sunday rice and peas. . . . All recipes for rice and peas are quite similar. This one is adapted from Island Cooking *by Dunstan Harris.*

In a large saucepan, combine the kidney beans, garlic, and water. Bring to a boil over medium-high heat, lower heat to medium-low and simmer, uncovered, until tender, about 2 hours. Add the salt, bacon, coconut milk, pepper, scallion, thyme, and chili. (Be careful to keep the chili intact; we want the flavor and aroma, not the heat.) Stir in the rice. Bring to a boil, reduce the heat to a simmer, cover, and cook for about 25 minutes, or until the liquid has been absorbed. Serve hot.

GUNGO PEAS AND RICE

Serves 6

6 slices bacon, diced
1 scallion, including green
    parts, diced
1 clove garlic, crushed
One 3-inch sprig fresh thyme,
    or 1½ teaspoons dried thyme
1 cup fresh gungo peas, or one
    16-ounce can pigeon peas
4 cups water (3 cups if using
    canned peas)
Salt and freshly ground
    pepper to taste
2 cups long-grain white rice

*Gungo (pronounced **goongo**) peas and rice is a delicacy at home. It was my mother's favorite dish, especially for Christmas. We would plant our peas during the month of September, as most Jamaicans do, to reap for Christmas. Gungo peas take about eight weeks to bear and have a wonderful green color when fresh. On the other islands, they are known as pigeon peas and are dried, but we like them fresh. If you cannot grow them in your locale, gungo peas are available in most markets, usually dried or canned.*

In a large Dutch oven, fry the bacon over medium heat for about 10 minutes, or until the fat has been released and the bacon is crisp. Add the scallion and garlic and sauté until translucent, about 1 minute. Add the thyme, peas, and water. Reduce heat to low and cook fresh peas, uncovered, for 1 to 2 hours, or until tender, adding more water if needed; cook canned pigeon peas for only 5 to 10 minutes. Add salt and pepper.

Add the rice, bring to a boil, and stir. Reduce the heat to a simmer, cover, and cook for about 20 minutes, or until the liquid is absorbed. Serve hot.

JERK BAKED BLACK BEANS
Serves 8 to 10

These beans are wonderful served alongside vegetables: try steamed squash, pumpkin, or spinach, or baked or boiled yams, sweet potatoes, or white potatoes. Or just spoon them over steamed rice.

....

12 ounces salt pork, slab bacon, or thick-cut bacon, diced
4 cups dried black beans, picked over, rinsed, and soaked overnight
6 cups water
1 onion, finely chopped
4 cloves garlic, minced
Two 18-ounce cans tomato sauce
4 tablespoons sugar
4 tablespoons Dry Jerk Seasoning (page 7)

....

In a slow cooker, combine the salt pork, beans, water, onion, garlic, tomato sauce, sugar, and jerk seasoning. Stir to blend. Cook on high until the liquid is bubbling, 15 to 20 minutes, then reduce the heat to low and cook for 6 to 8 hours, or until the beans are tender. Adjust the seasoning and serve.

SAUTÉED MUSHROOMS À LA JERK
Serves 4

This delicious side dish comes from my dear friend, Norma.

....

1 tablespoon unsalted butter
¼ cup olive oil
1 onion, finely chopped
1 pound mushrooms, stemmed and sliced (4 cups)
¼ cup dry white wine
2 tablespoons Dry Jerk Seasoning (page 7)
1 teaspoon Jerk Rub (page 7)
1 teaspoon fresh lemon juice
2 tablespoons minced fresh flat-leaf parsley (optional)

....

In a large, heavy skillet or sauté pan, melt the butter with the oil over medium heat. Add the onion and sauté until slightly softened, about 2 minutes. Add the mushrooms and sauté for 5 minutes, or until the mushrooms are rich brown in color. Stir in the wine, jerk seasoning, and jerk rub and continue cooking until most of the liquid has evaporated. Stir in the lemon juice, remove from the heat, sprinkle with the parsley if using, and serve.

JAMAICAN COLE SLAW
Serves 4 to 6

Cole slaw and barbecue make great companions. This version adds spice to give it a taste of Jamaica. To really go "island style," dice some pineapple and mango to mix into the cole slaw.

....

4 cups shredded cabbage
¾ cup shredded carrots
½ cup chopped toasted nuts (I like walnuts)
½ cup mayonnaise
2 tablespoons sugar
1 tablespoons cider vinegar
1 tablespoon Dry Jerk Seasoning (page 7)

....

In a large bowl, combine the cabbage, carrots, and nuts; set aside. In a separate bowl, mix together the mayonnaise, sugar, vinegar, and seasoning. Spoon over the cabbage mixture. Toss well. Cover and chill before serving.

AVOCADO AND PAPAYA GAZPACHO
Serves 6

This refreshing cold soup from the Busha Browne Company is spicy, sweet, and a perfect accompaniment to barbecued jerk meats on a hot summer day.

....

1 cup finely chopped papaya
1 cup finely chopped avocado
⅓ cup finely chopped green bell pepper
⅔ cup finely chopped tomatoes
¼ cup finely chopped sweet onion
3 cups tomato juice
3 cups unsweetened pineapple juice
   (preferably fresh)
1 teaspoon fresh lime or lemon juice
1 teaspoon hot pepper sauce, such as Busha
   Browne's Pukka Hot Pepper Sauce
Salt and freshly ground pepper to taste
Papaya seeds and cilantro sprigs for garnish

....

In a medium glass bowl, combine all the ingredients except the garnishes. Cover and refrigerate for at least 2 hours or up to 4 hours. Serve in chilled bowls, garnished with a few papaya seeds and a sprig of cilantro.

GRILLED PINEAPPLE
WITH PASSION FRUIT BUTTER

Serves 4

1 pineapple, green leaves
  still attached
3 tablespoons unsalted
  butter, melted
3 tablespoon Passion Fruit
  Sauce (page 152)
2 tablespoons chopped
  toasted cashews

Heat up your grill for delicious jerk chicken or pork, then cook this
delightful pineapple dish as an accompaniment.

....

Prepare a medium fire in a charcoal grill, or preheat a gas grill
to 350°F. Using a large knife, quarter the pineapple lengthwise
and cut out the core, leaving the green leaves on. Mix the melted
butter and passion fruit sauce together. Grill the pineapple on
one cut side until golden, about 5 minutes. Turn the fruit and
brush the cooked side with the passion fruit–butter sauce. Grill
the other cut side for 5 minutes, then brush with more of the
sauce mixture.

To serve, place the pineapple quarters on an attractive platter
and pour the remaining sauce over the top. Garnish with the
cashews. Each person should take a quarter and slice the fruit
away from the skin. Delicious!

VARIATION:
....

As an alternative to the cashews, try toasted coconut flakes.

6 pounds callaloo
2 tablespoons unsalted butter
3 onions, diced
2 tablespoons Dry Jerk
    Seasoning (page 7)
1 cup water
One 8-ounce can tomato sauce

Callaloo is a big, leafy green that is commonly available in Jamaica and many other Caribbean countries. If you are very lucky, a friend will bring it to you in big bunches when they come in from the country. Callaloo can often be found in West Indian groceries; if you can't locate any, you can substitute mustard greens or spinach. This recipe comes from my friend Eli Rickham.

Discard the outer leaves of the callaloo and wash the rest well in lots of water. Cut off the stalks and discard, and chop the leaves into small pieces.

In a large pot, melt the butter over medium heat. Add the onions and sauté until almost translucent, about 3 minutes. Add the dry jerk seasoning, water, and tomato sauce. Stir in the chopped callaloo. Reduce the heat to a simmer, cover, and cook for 15 to 20 minutes, until tender. Taste and adjust the seasoning. Serve hot.

HONEY-GINGER DIPPING SAUCE

Makes about 1¼ cups

One 8-ounce can sweetened
   tamarind nectar
1 tablespoon honey
2 to 3 inches fresh ginger,
   peeled and grated
1 tablespoons soy sauce
1 tablespoon Dry Jerk
   Seasoning (page 7)
1 teaspoon cornstarch
1 teaspoon water

This dipping sauce is delicious with all jerked meats and fish. Most of the sweetness is derived from the tamarind nectar. Cans of the nectar can be found in West Indian specialty foods stores or Asian food stores.

In a small saucepan, combine the tamarind nectar and honey. Bring to a boil and cook until reduced by one-third. Stir in the ginger, soy sauce, and dry jerk seasoning. Mix the cornstarch with the water to form a paste, then stir into the tamarind mixture. Cook, stirring constantly, until the sauce thickens, 1 to 2 minutes. Serve hot or at room temperature. To store, refrigerate in a tightly sealed glass jar. Use within 30 days; allow to come to room temperature for best flavor.

HONEY-SOY DIPPING SAUCE

Makes ¾ cup

This makes a great glaze for chicken legs and pork loin. Its flavor is similar to Chinese hoisin sauce.

....

3 tablespoons soy sauce
3 tablespoons honey
2 tablespoons red wine vinegar
1 teaspoon Dry Jerk Seasoning (page 7)
1½ teaspoons cornstarch
¼ cup water

....

In a small saucepan, combine the soy sauce, honey, vinegar, and jerk seasoning. Stir to blend, then bring to a boil. Mix together the cornstarch and the water. Stir into the sauce and cook, stirring constantly, until thickened, 1 to 2 minutes. Serve hot or at room temperature. Refrigerate in a tightly sealed glass jar. Use within 3 days; allow to come to room temperature for best flavor.

TAMARIND-APRICOT SAUCE

Makes about 1½ cups

This can be served as a condiment with meats.

....

1 (8-ounce) can sweetened tamarind nectar
4 ounces apricot jam
2 tablespoons honey
1 teaspoon Dijon-style mustard (optional)

....

In a small saucepan, combine the tamarind nectar and apricot jam and bring to a boil over medium heat. Continue to boil, stirring frequently, until the mixture thickens. Stir in the honey. Add the mustard if desired. Serve at room temperature. Refrigerate in a tightly sealed glass jar. Use within 3 days; allow to come to room temperature for best flavor.

FRESH MANGO CHUTNEY
WITH BANANA AND JERK SEASONING

Makes about 4 cups

¼ cup golden raisins
¼ cup water
½ cup firmly packed brown sugar
½ cup chopped onion
¾ cup cider vinegar
1 tablespoon Dry Jerk
   Seasoning (page 7)
Grated zest and juice of
   1 lime or lemon
1½ cups diced slightly underripe
   (green) mango
2 teaspoons hot pepper sauce
1 tablespoon Pickapeppa Sauce
1 teaspoon minced fresh ginger
1 ripe banana, diced

This chutney is delicious with pork, chicken, fish, or shrimp. Pickapeppa Sauce is a classic Jamaican condiment made with tamarind, tomatoes, mangoes, onions, peppers, and spices. It's widely available in supermarkets.

Soak the raisins in hot water to plump for about 30 minutes, then drain.

In a nonaluminum saucepan, combine the water, sugar, onion, and vinegar. Bring to a boil and stir in the dry jerk seasoning, lime zest and juice, mango, hot sauce, Pickapeppa Sauce, and ginger. Reduce the heat and simmer, uncovered. for 30 minutes, or until thickened. Stir in the plumped raisins and banana. Cover and refrigerate for at least 2 hours before serving. Store in the refrigerator for up to 2 weeks.

CHAPTER 7

DESSERTS

Picture this. It is lunch break at school and the students tumble out of the classrooms by the hundreds. The street vendors are poised and ready to make their sales to the youngsters. They have glass and wooden cases, which they unload from buses and cars, along with the baskets carried on their heads. In the cases are the delights that are as basic to Jamaica as jerk chicken: totoes, gizadas, sweet potato pudding, bullas, plantain tarts, and paradise plum. Instead of buying a balanced lunch as instructed by their mothers, the children descend upon the vendors with an appetite for pure sweets.

Some of these sweets you can make yourself in your own home; others you must come to Jamaica to try. The names may be unfamiliar, but the sweets are not terribly exotic. A gizada, for instance, is a coconut tartlet—delicious and chewy.

A bulla is a wonderful, filling sweet made of water, sugar, and flour. Paradise plums are red and yellow hard rock candy, colored to look like our native plums. In this chapter, you will find recipes for totoes (a kind of bar cookie), gizadas, and plantain tarts, as well as fancier desserts.

You see, in the hotels, one finds gourmet desserts all based on tropical fruits but prepared in the European manner, such as guava tarts and trifles. Some of these desserts are as easy to make as combining slices of mango with vanilla ice cream. Top with a rum-flavored custard, and you have a heavenly dessert.

None of the desserts in this chapter are served at jerk shacks, but they are featured in every Jamaican household on a Sunday and at buffets where jerk is one of the highlights—and in every school cafeteria and at many roadside stands.

When yu go a firesidean' see food, eat halfan' lef' half.

JAMAICAN FRUIT SALAD
Serves 8

Instead of having a cookie for a snack, Jamaicans eat fruit salad, made with seasonal fruits. But don't add bananas until just before serving, as they will turn dark if left to sit for very long. Serve the salad as is, or with vanilla ice cream.

....

2 mangoes
4 oranges
2 medium papayas
1 pineapple
Juice of 2 limes or lemons
2 bananas

....

Peel all the fruits. Remove the seeds from the mangoes, oranges, and the papayas. Core the pineapple. Cut all the fruits into bite-sized pieces and put them in a bowl. Squeeze the limes over all the fruits and mix together. Just before serving, peel and slice the bananas and stir them into the salad.

BAKED BANANAS WITH TAMARIND SAUCE
Serves 4

This can be served as a dessert, by itself or without ice cream, or as a side dish to accompany meats.

....

4 ripe bananas
¼ cup Tamarind-Apricot Sauce (page 128)
¼ cup sweetened flaked coconut
¼ cup slivered almonds
1 tablespoon packed brown sugar
2 tablespoons unsalted butter, melted
Juice of 1 lime or lemon

....

Preheat the oven to 350°F. Peel the bananas and split lengthwise. Arrange in a buttered shallow casserole dish. Spoon the tamarind-apricot sauce over the bananas, then sprinkle with the coconut and almonds. Mix the brown sugar with the melted butter and lime juice, and pour over the bananas. Bake ripe bananas for 20 minutes; if the bananas are not very ripe, bake for 30 minutes. Serve hot.

TROPICAL TRIFLE
Serves 8 to 10

In the early 1970s, my husband and I catered a private dinner party and then a large reception in honor of a visit by Queen Elizabeth. How proud I was as I prepared the dinner for one hundred of Jamaica's finest citizens and the royal party. I was determined to serve the best and sweetest mangoes in a variation of trifle that I felt sure would impress the Queen and her entire party. Only I did not plan on the electricity going out that very day. What a mess! Luckily, I had friends at the Kingshouse facilities (which had a battery-powered generator) and they came through for me to finish the trifle of trifles. (Yes, it was a smashing success.)

The classic dish to prepare this in is a clear, round footed dish with sides about 7 to 8 inches high.

Three 12-ounce cans
    evaporated milk
4 cups whole milk
1 cup sugar, plus 2 tablespoons
6 large egg yolks, lightly beaten
2 tablespoons sweet sherry
1 teaspoon vanilla extract
1 cup sliced fresh strawberries
About twelve 1-inch-thick
    slices day-old pound cake;
    or 24 ladyfingers, halved;
    or 36 macaroons
2 or 3 mangoes, peeled, pitted,
    and sliced
4 or 5 kiwifruits, peeled
    and sliced
1 cup seedless grapes,
    preferably red, halved

In a double boiler, heat both the milks over low heat, then add the 1 cup sugar. Cook over simmering water, stirring occasionally, until bubbles appear and the sugar dissolves. In a bowl, mix a little of the hot milk mixture into the beaten egg yolks and then return all of it to the double boiler. Cook for about 15 minutes, stirring constantly, until it thickens enough to coat the back of a spoon. Do not allow it to boil, or it will separate. Stir in the sherry and vanilla. Remove from the heat, set the pan in a bowl of ice water, and stir frequently to cool.

In a small bowl, combine the strawberries with the 2 tablespoons sugar and stir to coat; set aside.

Line a trifle dish (or any clear, deep dish) with slices of cake, ladyfingers, or macaroons. Pour half the cooled custard over the cake, then add half of the strawberries, mangoes, and kiwifruit. Add another layer of cake or cookies and top with the remaining custard, then the fruit. Cover and refrigerate for at least 4 hours or up to 12 hours. Serve by large spoonfuls.

VARIATION:

If you are serving to adults only, you may want to sprinkle a little extra sherry over each layer of cake or cookies. I love trifle this way, but trifle is always so popular with children that I seldom get to serve it with the extra sherry.

JAMAICA LIME PIE

Serves 6

FILLING

4 large egg yolks
1 large egg white
One 14-ounce can sweetened
  condensed milk
½ cup fresh lime juice
¼ teaspoon salt
One partially baked 9-inch pie
  crust (page 153), chilled

MERINGUE

3 large egg whites
½ teaspoon cream of tartar
6 tablespoons sugar

Although the lime is very important to Jamaica, almost more basic to our cuisine is the condensed milk also found in this recipe. All Jamaicans use evaporated and sweetened condensed milk. Not only is canned milk more reliable in a land with unreliable electricity, it is considered a great delicacy.

Our local limes resemble the very tart, wild Key lime found on the Florida Keys. However, it is difficult to find these off the island, so this recipe uses the more common Persian lime, readily available in U.S. markets. This is delicious with a cup of Blue Mountain coffee for dessert.

To make the filling: In a medium bowl, beat the egg yolks and egg white until they are very thick and lemon-colored. Stir in the condensed milk, lime juice, and salt until well blended. Pour into the chilled pie shell. Refrigerate for several hours to allow the filling to set.

Shortly before serving, make the meringue: Preheat the oven to 425°F. In a large bowl, beat the 3 egg whites with the cream of tartar until they form soft peaks. Gradually beat in the sugar, and continue beating until it is dissolved. By then the meringue should be stiff and glossy. Spread over the filling, being sure to seal the edges well so that the meringue will not shrink.

Bake for 5 to 7 minutes, or until delicately browned. Let cool away from drafts.

WHITE CHOCOLATE PASSION

Serves 8 to 10

4 ounces white chocolate, chopped

¼ cup Passion Fruit Sauce (page 152)

¼ cup water

3 dozen ripe fresh strawberries or bite-sized pieces of fruit of your choice

This delicious fondue of white chocolate and passion fruit is beautiful and adapts well to entertaining large or small groups. Surround the bowl of warm sauce with attractively arranged fruits. This is also particularly good with mangoes, papayas, pears, and apples.

In a double boiler over barely simmering water, melt the chocolate. (Or, to melt in a microwave, cook at very low heat, not more than 30 percent power. Stir often.)

Mix the passion fruit sauce with the water, then stir this mixture into the melted white chocolate until smooth.

To serve, place the fondue in an attractive bowl surrounded by fruit on a platter. Don't forget the skewers or food picks!

COFFEE MOUSSE
Serves 6

½ cup heavy cream
¾ cup sugar
¼ cup cold water
1 tablespoon unflavored gelatin
¼ cup hot water
2 tablespoons instant coffee
   powder, preferably espresso
4 large egg whites
2 ounces semisweet
   chocolate, grated

This delicious coffee mousse will make you believe you are having dessert on the veranda of a luxurious estate in Jamaica. Serve in your prettiest footed dessert bowls or parfait glasses, with coconut cookies alongside.

In a deep bowl, beat the cream with ¼ cup of the sugar until soft peaks form. Set aside.

Pour the cold water into a small bowl. Sprinkle the gelatin over the water and stir well to dissolve. Allow to sit until translucent, about 3 minutes. Add the hot water and the coffee powder and stir well until dissolved. Fold in the whipped cream. In a large bowl, beat the egg whites until soft peaks form, then add the remaining ½ cup sugar. Beat constantly until stiff, glossy peaks form.

Fold the beaten egg whites into the whipped cream. Fold in the grated chocolate. Refrigerate for 4 hours. To serve, spoon into individual bowls or parfait glasses.

COLD COFFEE SOUFFLÉ

Serves 6 to 8

1½ cups cold brewed coffee

⅔ cup sugar

1 tablespoon unflavored gelatin

½ cup milk

3 large eggs, separated

¼ teaspoon salt

1 teaspoon vanilla extract

Whipped cream for garnish

Coffee bean candies for
   garnish (optional)

This makes a delightful centerpiece for a dessert table. I use my fanciest mold and Jamaican Blue Mountain coffee, of course!

In a medium saucepan, combine the coffee, ⅓ cup of the sugar, the gelatin, and milk. Cook over low heat, stirring occasionally, until the gelatin is dissolved. In a separate bowl, lightly beat the egg yolks with the remaining ⅓ cup sugar and the salt. In a bowl, whisk a little of the hot milk mixture into the beaten egg yolk mixture and then return all of it to the pan. Continue to cook over low heat, stirring frequently, until the mixture thickens slightly. Remove from the heat and stir in the vanilla. Let cool, stirring often. Meanwhile, beat the egg whites in a large bowl until soft peaks form. When the milk–egg yolk mixture begins to set, after about 5 minutes, fold the beaten egg whites into the mixture until blended. Pour into a decorative 3-cup mold. Cover and refrigerate until set, at least 4 hours.

To serve, soak a clean kitchen towel in warm water, wring out, and wrap around the mold for 2 or 3 minutes to loosen the soufflé. Invert the mold onto a plate to unmold and garnish with whipped cream and coffee bean candies, if desired.

BREAD PUDDING

Serves 6 to 8

1 pound day-old white sandwich
   bread, crusts removed
½ cup sugar
¾ teaspoon ground cinnamon
¼ teaspoon ground nutmeg
⅓ cup light or dark rum
½ cup raisins
4 tablespoons unsalted butter,
   melted
½ cup sweetened condensed milk
4 cups whole milk
5 large eggs, well beaten

This bread pudding is a favorite of my father. It rises beautifully in the oven, turns a wonderful golden brown, and yields a creamy consistency. The condensed milk gives it a rich, smooth taste, just barely flavored with the rum. This is delicious with ice cream, whipped cream, Rum Custard (page 152), or hard sauce.

Preheat the oven to 350°F. Grease an 8- or 9-inch square baking dish.

Cut the bread into 1-inch dice or tear into small pieces. In a large bowl, mix together the bread, sugar, cinnamon, nutmeg, rum, raisins, and melted butter. Pour into the baking dish. Place the dish on a sided baking sheet.

In a medium bowl, combine the condensed milk, whole milk, and eggs and pour over the bread mixture. Bake for 1 to 1¼ hours, or until a knife inserted in the center comes out clean. Serve warm or cooled.

JAMAICAN CORN PONE
Serves 8

2¾ cups cornmeal
⅓ cup all-purpose flour
6 cups coconut milk
2⅔ cups firmly packed
   brown sugar
1 tablespoon vanilla extract
¼ cup light or dark rum
1⅓ cups raisins

TOPPING
1 cup coconut milk
½ cup firmly packed brown sugar
4 tablespoons unsalted butter,
   melted

Whipped cream for garnish

My friend Norma Benghiat, with whom I went to school, is one of Jamaica's leading food researchers and the author of several articles and cookbooks. This is her version of the corn pone made by the early settlers in the American colonies. Their corn pone was a plain corn cake baked in the oven. As you will see, the Jamaican corn pone is a delightful pudding. Your family will enjoy it as either a dessert or a snack.

Preheat the oven to 300°F. Grease a 9- by-13-inch baking dish.

Combine the cornmeal and flour in a bowl. Stir in the coconut milk, a little at a time, to make a smooth batter. Stir in the sugar, vanilla, rum, and raisins. The mixture should be liquid rather than thick. Pour into the baking dish and bake for at least 1 hour, or when set and a knife blade inserted into the center comes out clean. Remove from the oven (leaving the oven on) and let cool for about 1 hour, or until the pone is slightly firm but still warm.

To make the topping: In a small bowl, combine all the ingredients. Pour over the pone. Bake for another 30 minutes, or until a toothpick inserted into the center comes out clean.

Let cool for 30 minutes before spooning into bowls and serving garnished with whipped cream.

PLANTAIN TARTLETS

Makes 8 tartlets

3 very ripe, black plantains
½ cup sugar, plus more for garnish
¼ to ½ teaspoon ground nutmeg
  (to taste)
¼ teaspoon vanilla extract, or
  up to 1 teaspoon to taste
1 or 2 drops red food coloring
  (optional)
2 recipes Pie Crust (page 153)

These tartlets and the gizadas that follow are favorites of Jamaican schoolchildren.

....

Peel the plantains. Boil in water to cover until tender, about 15 minutes. Drain, transfer to a bowl, and mash until smooth. Add the ½ cup sugar, the nutmeg, vanilla, and red food coloring, if you like.

Preheat the oven to 400°F. On a lightly floured board, roll out the dough to two 12- to 14-inch rounds. Using a can, glass, or cup 4 to 5 inches in diameter, cut out 4 rounds. Repeat with the second disk of dough.

Place 1 tablespoon of the filling on half of each of the dough rounds, leaving a ¼-inch border. Fold the other half over to form a half circle, then crimp the edges with a fork. Sprinkle with sugar.

Bake on ungreased baking sheets for 30 to 40 minutes, or until the crust is golden brown. Transfer from the baking sheets to wire racks. Serve warm or at room temperature.

GIZADAS

Makes about 4 dozen

1 ripe coconut, peeled and grated (see page 12), or one 7-ounce bag sweetened grated frozen or dry coconut

⅔ cup firmly packed brown sugar

½ teaspoon ground nutmeg

Pie Crust (page 153)

Chopped toasted nuts, such as almonds, macadamias, or pecans, for garnish (optional)

Gizadas, oh gizadas—do they bring back memories from my childhood! As I have told you, every child in Jamaica buys from the sweets maker, and the gizada is high on the list of favorite treats! The coconut filling becomes almost chewy when cooked like this.

If you can't find a ripe coconut and have a choice between dry or frozen coconut, choose the frozen. It is closer in taste and texture to fresh coconut.

....

Preheat the oven to 375°F. Lightly grease 2 baking sheets. In a medium bowl, mix together the coconut, brown sugar, and nutmeg thoroughly. Set aside.

On a lightly floured board, roll the dough out ⅛ inch thick and use a 2- or 2½-inch cookie or biscuit cutter to cut into rounds. Place 1 teaspoonful of the coconut mixture in the center of each round. Fold up the dough around the coconut filling to make a bowl, pinching it into place. Place the gizadas on the baking sheets and bake until browned, about 20 minutes. Transfer to wire racks to cool slightly; these are best served warm with chopped toasted nuts for garnish.

TOTOES
Makes 9 squares

2 cups all-purpose flour
2 teaspoons baking powder
1 teaspoon ground cinnamon
½ teaspoon ground nutmeg
4 tablespoons unsalted butter,
    at room temperature
½ cup granulated sugar
½ cup firmly packed brown sugar
1 large egg, beaten
2 teaspoons vanilla extract
About ½ cup milk

A favorite with children, these cookies are easily made and use ingredients you probably keep on hand.

Preheat the oven to 375°F. Grease an 8-inch square pan.

In a medium bowl, combine the flour, baking powder, cinnamon, and nutmeg. Stir with a whisk to blend. In a large bowl, cream the butter and sugars together until light and fluffy; gradually stir in the flour mixture. Stir in the beaten egg, vanilla, and just enough milk to make a stiff cookie dough batter.

Spread the batter in the prepared pan. Bake for 30 to 35 minutes, or until evenly golden brown. Let cool completely and cut into squares. Store leftovers in an airtight container.

BANANA BREAD

Makes 1 loaf; serves 10 to 12

2 ripe bananas
1 teaspoon fresh lemon juice
½ cup vegetable shortening
1 cup sugar
2 large eggs
2 cups all-purpose flour
1 tablespoon baking powder
½ teaspoon salt
1 cup chopped nuts (optional)
2 teaspoons packed brown
   sugar mixed with ¼ teaspoon
   ground cinnamon

I usually double this recipe and freeze the second loaf. This is delicious at teatime!

Preheat the oven to 350°F. Grease a 9- by-5-inch loaf pan.

Peel and mash enough bananas to make 1 cup mashed banana. Immediately stir in the lemon juice to prevent browning. In a large bowl, cream the shortening and sugar together until light and fluffy. Stir in the eggs and cream until blended, then stir in the mashed banana.

In a medium bowl, combine the flour, baking powder, and salt. Stir with a whisk to blend. Mix quickly into the banana mixture. Add the nuts, if desired.

Pour the mixture into the loaf pan and bake for about 1¼ hours, or until a cake tester inserted in the center comes out clean. As soon as you take the banana bread from the oven, sprinkle with the brown sugar mixture to make a beautiful glaze. Let cool in the pan on a wire rack for about 10 minutes, then unmold from the pan. Return to the wire rack to cool completely.

HONEY PINEAPPLE BREAD

Makes 1 loaf; serves 10 to 12

2 tablespoons vegetable oil
1 cup honey
1 large egg
2¼ cups all-purpose flour
1 tablespoon baking powder
½ teaspoon salt
¾ cup chopped nuts
1 cup wheat bran
1 cup canned pineapple juice

Not only does the bran in this recipe add delicious texture to the bread, it also adds healthy fiber to your diet.

Preheat the oven to 350°F. Grease a 9- by-5-inch loaf pan.

In a large bowl, stir the oil and honey together, then add the egg and mix well. In a medium bowl, combine the flour, baking powder, and salt. Stir with a whisk to blend. Mix ½ cup of the flour mixture with the nuts. Add about half of the remaining flour mixture to the egg mixture and stir well. Stir in the bran and pineapple juice, then all the remaining flour and the nut-flour mixture.

Pour into the prepared pan and bake for 1¼ hours, or until a cake tester inserted in the center comes out clean. Let cool in the pan on a wire rack for about 10 minutes, then remove from the pan. Return to the wire rack to cool completely.

QUICK ORANGE BREAD

Makes 1 loaf; serves 10 to 12

2 cups all-purpose flour
4 teaspoons baking powder
⅓ cup sugar
½ teaspoon salt
2 large eggs
½ cup fresh orange juice
3 tablespoons unsalted butter, melted
½ cup chopped candied orange peel
½ teaspoon grated orange zest

Because of our British heritage, Jamaicans still enjoy afternoon tea. Usually we serve toast with guava jelly and a piece of this type of sweet, cakelike bread. By the way, a cup of coffee is equally acceptable at teatime!

Preheat the oven to 350°F. Grease a 9- by-5-inch loaf pan.

In a medium bowl, combine the flour, baking powder, sugar, and salt. Stir with a whisk to blend. In a large bowl, beat the eggs well and stir in the orange juice, melted butter, orange peel, and orange zest. Stir the flour mixture into the egg mixture just to blend; do not overmix.

Pour into the prepared pan and bake for 1 hour, or until a cake tester inserted in the center comes out clean. Let cool in the pan on a wire rack for about 10 minutes, then remove from the pan. Return to the wire rack to cool completely.

RUM CUSTARD
Makes about 2 cups; serves 4

Serve this delicious custard over fresh fruits, such as mango, pineapple, papaya, or banana. It is also wonderful as a topping for cake or ice cream.

....

1½ cups milk
¼ cup firmly packed light brown sugar
⅛ teaspoon salt
3 large egg yolks, lightly beaten
2 tablespoons dark rum

....

In a double boiler, combine the milk, brown sugar, and salt. Cook over simmering water, stirring occasionally, until bubbles appear and the sugar dissolves.

Mix a little of the hot milk mixture into the beaten egg yolks and then return all of it to the double boiler. Cook for about 15 minutes, stirring constantly, until it thickens enough to coat the back of a spoon. Do not allow it to boil, or it will separate.

Remove from the heat and let cool slightly, then stir in the rum. Cover and let cool to room temperature, then chill thoroughly before serving.

PASSION FRUIT SAUCE
Makes about 1½ cups

If this recipe seems too complicated, there is a commercially prepared passion fruit sauce available in the American market. Passion fruit is similar to tamarind in its extreme acidity. You will certainly want to dilute the pulp before tasting. This versatile sauce is used in several recipes in this chapter; it is also delicious served over fresh fruit, or as a base for a seafood sauce.

....

2 passion fruits
1 cup sugar
1 cup water

....

Halve the passion fruits, and then scoop out the pulp and seeds. Discard the skin. In a medium saucepan, combine all the ingredients and bring to a boil, then reduce the heat to a simmer. Cook, stirring occasionally, until the pulp is soft, about 15 minutes. Set a sieve over a bowl and press the pulp through, then discard the seeds and solids left in the sieve. Let the strained sauce cool to room temperature before using. Store in the refrigerator in a tightly covered container for up to 2 weeks. Bring back to room temperature before serving.

PIE CRUST

Makes one 9-inch pie shell

1 cup all-purpose flour
½ teaspoon salt
⅓ cup vegetable shortening or
    lard (look for nonhydrogenated
    shortening)
3 tablespoons ice water

My mother almost never cooked—but she sure knew how to make a good pie crust.

In a medium bowl, combine the flour and salt. Stir with a whisk to blend. Cut the shortening into the flour mixture with a pastry blender or 2 dinner knives until the particles are about the size of dried peas.

Add the water gradually, a few drops at a time, tossing the dough lightly with a fork to be sure that the water is distributed evenly. Gather the dough together to form a ball. Handle the dough as little as possible after adding the water. This will help keep it flaky and tender. Form the dough into a disk and refrigerate for at least 30 minutes.

UNBAKED PIE SHELL: To make a pie shell, roll out the dough on a lightly floured surface, forming a round about 12 inches in diameter. Carefully transfer the dough to a 9-inch pie pan. Trim overhanging dough to 1 inch, fold it under, and crimp the edges.

PARTIALLY BAKED PIE SHELL: Preheat the oven 450°F. Prepare the pie shell as for an unbaked pie shell, above. Prick the pie shell all over with a fork. Line the shell with a sheet of parchment paper or aluminum foil and fill with pie weights or dried beans. Bake for about 8 minutes, or until set. Remove the foil or paper and weights or beans and bake for an additional 2 to 4 minutes, or until lightly browned. Cool before filling.

CHAPTER 8

DRINKS

Jamaica, as everyone knows, is world famous for its Blue Mountain coffee. The soil in the higher altitudes of the Blue Mountains produces coffee that many people consider to be the best anywhere. There are many delicious ways to enjoy Jamaican coffee, including my favorite, Calypso Coffee, which is found in this chapter.

Because of our British heritage, Jamaicans are also big tea drinkers. For a spot o' tea, we all take a break around four in the afternoon. Although the climate is hot, we learned from that other great English colony, India, to wear loose, lightweight clothing and to eat spicy foods and drink hot beverages to make us sweat. The evaporating perspiration makes us feel cooler.

In our houses there is always tea—real tea, not the "sissy" tea bags, or even the little tea balls, but real loose tea that is strained through beautiful silver strainers in the fancier homes, or through plain metal strainers in the simpler houses. Our tea is usually imported from India by way of

Great Britain. Herbal teas are also very popular, especially because you can just step outside your front door and pick a handful of herbs from your garden.

Of course, the popularity of tea is good news for our foremost local tea leaf reader, Mrs. Delgado. You will still see a long line of cars at her doorstep every afternoon. Her visitors are mostly politicians who think her advice is critical for their political survival, or ladies who are curious about the nocturnal activities of their husbands!

When I go to visit my friend Eli, she always has a beautiful tray waiting, set with a pot of tea, toast with guava jelly, banana bread, scones, coconut biscuits, or a light sandwich. In my mother's day, we had wonderful tea parties, with Blue Willow dishes from China. Sometimes we would read the tea leaves.

In general, the ladies of Jamaica, as the women like to be called, are not big drinkers of alcohol. The men, however, seem to make up for us. You will see men sitting around the jerk shacks playing our national game, dominoes, drinking "whites" after "whites." A "whites," always referred to in the plural, is a stiff mix of high-proof white rum and water. Truly a potent drink.

Then we have the ever-famous rum punch served at all parties and gatherings. The rule of thumb is to mix 1 portion of sour, 2 portions of sweet, 3 portions of strong, and 4 portions of weak. With this little rhyme, you can mix up many variations, depending on what you have on hand. A typical punch might contain lime juice (sour), grenadine syrup (sweet), rum (strong), and another fruit juice, such as orange juice (weak). I like a touch of freshly grated nutmeg as a garnish.

When you go to Jamaica, you will see that coconuts provide one of the main drinks of the island. The coconuts are picked much younger than those that you see in the States. Indeed, the coconuts are so young that they still have their green husks on. Coconut meat of mature coconuts is not like the meat of the young coconuts sold in Jamaica. In these, the meat is a jellylike substance and the coconut water is pure and sweet. Folklore says this coconut water is the best cure for kidney problems and high blood pressure.

Along the roadsides in Jamaica, you will see mounds of fresh coconuts being prepared by the coconut man with his machete. When I was a child, the coconut man would pass by the house on his dray, pulled by donkeys and filled with coconuts. He would shout, "Coconut, coconut!" We would shout back "Coconut man, coconut man!" and he would know to stop. We would rush out to the gate and try to climb on the dray to select our coconut. Then the coconut man would chop a little hole in the husk and give it to the buyer, who held the enormous coconut to his or her mouth and drank and drank. Ah . . . what a thirst quencher!

When we were finished, we'd hand the coconut back to the coconut man, who deftly chopped out a thin slice of the shell with his machete, then quickly chopped open the nut. We'd scrape the inside of the nut with the coconut spoon supplied by the coconut man and devour all the jelly. This is the healthiest food there is. At home, we always had a jug of coconut water and a bowl of coconut jelly in the refrigerator.

We also had the custom, left over from colonial times, of having drinks in the late afternoon. My mother was fond of rum and ginger, and she would lift her glass and say "Chin-chin" to anyone who was with her.

Nuh cup nuh bruk,

nuh coffee nuh dash wey.

RUM AND COCONUT WATER
Serves 1

This is the Jamaican man's drink. After Hurricane Gilbert in 1988, when there were few coconuts left on the north coast of the island, my husband had a very difficult time trying to get his favorite cure-all. If you can't get a whole young coconut or don't want to take a hammer and nail to a coconut to drain it, coconut water is available online and in stores that sell Caribbean or Southeast Asian ingredients.

1 whole young coconut
2 ounces white rum
1 dash bitters (optional)

With a large, clean nail and a hammer, knock 3 holes into the coconut, through the 3 visible "eyes" on the coconut, and place hole side down over a glass bowl big enough to hold the coconut up as the water drips out. When the coconut water has drained out, you should have enough to fill a 6- to 8-ounce glass. Stir in the rum and bitters, if using, and serve.

158

ISLAND COFFEE

Serves 6 to 8

2 oranges, scrubbed
4 sugar cubes
⅔ cup heavy cream
⅔ cup confectioners' sugar
2 tablespoons unsalted butter
¼ cup granulated sugar
½ cup brandy
5 tablespoons Grand Marnier
   or other orange liqueur
4 cups hot brewed coffee,
   preferably Jamaican Blue
   Mountain coffee

This delicious coffee will make you think of the most elegant restaurants on the islands. It does take a few minutes to make the garnishes from the oranges, but the final effect is worth the effort.

Rub both oranges with the sugar cubes to get some of the oil from the orange peel onto the sugar. Cut 6 to 8 thin strips of zest from 1 orange and reserve for garnish. Cut the orange in half and squeeze out the juice. Cut the other orange into very thin slices.

In a deep bowl, beat the cream with the confectioners' sugar until soft peaks form. Set aside.

In a large saucepan, melt the butter with the granulated sugar over low heat. Stir in the sugar cubes and orange juice until the sugar has dissolved. Stir in the brandy and liqueur. Light a long-handled match, avert your face, and light the liquid. Shake the pan until the flames subside.

Pour the hot coffee into your prettiest mugs or footed coffee cups and then add the orange mixture to taste, as well as a strip of orange zest. Garnish with the whipped cream and a slice of orange.

CALYPSO COFFEE
Serves 4

Calypso coffee, a mixture of our famous Blue Mountain coffee, dark rum, and coffee liqueur, is a drink that is sure to enhance your holiday season!

....

2 cups hot Jamaican Blue Mountain coffee
1 tablespoon sugar
1 ounce Jamaican dark rum
3 ounces Tia Maria or other coffee liqueur
Whipped cream for garnish
Zest of 1 lime, cut into thin strips with a zester, for garnish

....

In a medium saucepan, heat the coffee just to simmering. Stir in the sugar, rum, and liqueur. Pour into large mugs or footed coffee glasses. Garnish with whipped cream and lime zest. Serve at once.

GRAPEFRUIT JUICE AND RUM
Serves 4

I prefer the sweeter, ruby-red grapefruit juice for this drink—and it keeps its beautiful color especially well with the light rum. You can use regular grapefruit juice, but it may be too tart.

....

4 cups grapefruit juice
4 ounces very light rum
Ice cubes for serving
4 maraschino cherries

....

Pour 1 cup of grapefruit juice and 1 ounce of rum into each of 4 tall glasses and stir to blend. Add lots of ice to fill the glass, and top with a cherry. Very refreshing!

PASSION FRUIT MARTINI
Serves 1

Passion fruit nectar is available in many specialty food shops, Caribbean markets, and even supermarkets.

....

Crushed ice for shaking
1½ ounces citrus-flavored vodka or rum
1½ ounces Cointreau liqueur
1 ounce passion fruit nectar
Sliced mango, kiwi, or pineapple, for garnish
   (optional)

....

In a cocktail shaker filled with crushed ice, combine the vodka or rum, Cointreau, and passion fruit nectar. Shake thoroughly and strain into a martini glass. Garnish with the sliced tropical fruit, if desired, and serve.

THE BLUE LAGOON
Serves 2

The lovely blue-green color of this drink reminds me of tranquil Caribbean waters.

....

2 cups ice
1½ ounces vanilla rum
¾ ounce Grand Marnier
1½ ounces blue curaçao
6 ounces pineapple juice
Pineapple slices for garnish

....

Place the ice in a blender and add the vanilla rum, Grand Marnier, blue curaçao, and pineapple juice. Blend until the ice is a slushy consistency and pour into two large (10- to 12-ounce) martini glasses garnished with pineapple slices.

BLOODY MARY À LA JERK
Serves 6 to 8

This is a brilliant island twist on the classic morning-after pick-me-up, using rum rather than vodka and spicing it up with jerk seasoning.

....

4 cups tomato juice
½ cup fresh lime or lemon juice
1 tablespoon Dry Jerk Seasoning (page 7)
1 cup light or dark rum
Generous dashes of hot pepper sauce to taste
Celery sticks and lime wedges for garnish

....

In a medium saucepan, combine the tomato juice, lime or lemon juice, and dry jerk seasoning. Bring to a boil over medium heat.

Remove from the heat and let cool. Stir in the rum and pepper sauce. Pour into a pitcher and refrigerate for at least 2 hours to chill. Serve over ice in tall glasses, garnished with celery sticks and lime wedges.

FROZEN DAIQUIRIS
Serves 4

A daiquiri, to my mind, is one of the most romantic of drinks. This semifrozen slush usually is served in a shallow Champagne glass, garnished with a cherry, a sprig of mint, and pieces of mango or some other fruit. As most Americans know, daiquiris are made from fresh fruits with rum and ice. The pastel colors of the drink vary, depending on the fruit or juice that flavors it.

....

3 cups crushed ice
6 ounces light rum
¼ cup Triple Sec
¼ cup Simple Syrup (page 170), or
    2 tablespoons superfine sugar
1 ounce fresh lime juice
Orange slices and maraschino cherries
    for garnish

....

In a blender, combine the crushed ice with the rum, Triple Sec, simple syrup or sugar, and lime juice. Blend for about 30 seconds, or until slushy. Pour into shallow Champagne glasses and serve with small drink straws. Garnish each drink with an orange slice and a cherry.

FROZEN MANGO-PEACH DAIQUIRIS

Serves 2 to 4

I spend some of my time in Georgia, where I have a second home, and this wonderful concoction combines Jamaican rum and mango with my beloved Georgia peaches.

....

Crushed ice
1 cup peeled, sliced mango, plus 2 to
    4 additional slices for garnish
1 cup peeled, sliced fresh peaches, plus
    2 to 4 additional slices for garnish
½ cup light rum
¼ cup superfine sugar
Juice of 1 lime or lemon

....

Fill a blender three-fourths full with ice, then add the other ingredients. Blend until slushy. Pour into shallow Champagne glasses to serve and garnish with slices of peach and mango.

REFRESHING RUM DRINK

Serves 2

This is wonderful in extremely hot weather—say, after a long day on a pineapple plantation tour.

....

Crushed ice for shaking
3 ounces white rum
1 ounce fresh lime juice
1 tablespoon Simple Syrup (page 170)
Club soda, well chilled
Lime wedges for garnish

....

Fill a cocktail shaker with ice. Add the rum, lime juice, and simple syrup. Cap, shake well, and strain into 2 tall glasses filled with crushed ice. Fill the rest of the way with club soda and garnish with lime wedges.

RUM PUNCH
Serves 16 to 20

Remember the formula for a perfect rum punch:
1 portion of sour, 2 portions of sweet, 3 portions
of strong, 4 portions of weak. This looks beautiful
served in a punch bowl with a pretty ice ring
layered with orange slices and cherry halves.

....

1 cup fresh lime or lemon juice (sour)
2 cups grenadine syrup (sweet)
2 cups Jamaican white rum (strong)
1 cup light rum (strong)
2 cups pineapple juice (weak)
2 cups orange juice (weak)
½ teaspoon freshly grated nutmeg

....

In a large pitcher, combine all the ingredients.
Stir to blend, and refrigerate for at least 1 hour
before serving.

MANGO-PAPAYA PUNCH
Serves 8 to 10

The blending of these two tropical fruits crates the type of drink that island crooners write songs about!

....

1 small papaya, peeled, seeded, and chopped
One 19-ounce can mango nectar
1 cup sugar
3 cups water
Juice of 2 limes
4 cups club soda
3 ounces light rum (optional)

....

In a blender, combine the papaya, mango nectar, sugar, water, and lime juice. Process for about 30 seconds, or until well blended. Refrigerate for at least 1 hour. Stir in the club soda and rum just before serving. Serve in your most attractive punch cups. If possible, decorate the punch bowl with hibiscus or other blossoms.

TROPICAL FRUIT PUNCH
Serves 8

This nonalcoholic punch is a favorite of children for picnics. Feel free to spike it with light rum for the grown-ups.

....

2 cups fresh orange juice
2 cups pineapple juice
1 cup guava juice
1½ cups club soda
Grated fresh nutmeg to taste

....

In a large pitcher, combine all the ingredients and stir to blend. Refrigerate for at least 1 hour, then enjoy.

MARION'S FRUIT PICK-ME-UP

Serves 12

I would rather have this yummy liquid concoction than a regular lunch any day. We always bought fresh fruit on a Saturday morning. On the following Friday, if all the fruit had not been eaten, it was put into the blender and made into a rich drink for everyone. Delicious and very nutritious.

....

2 ripe bananas, peeled
½ very, very ripe papaya, peeled, seeded, and chopped (about 2 cups)
2 very ripe mangoes, peeled, pitted, and chopped (about 2 cups)
Juice of 2 limes
One 14-ounce can sweetened condensed milk
½ cup water
3 cups pineapple juice
One 46-ounce can tropical fruit punch
Ice cubes for serving
Freshly grated nutmeg for garnish

....

In a blender, combine all the ingredients except the ice and nutmeg. Process until smooth. Serve with lots of ice and a grating of fresh nutmeg on top.

PINEAPPLE FRAPPÉ

Serves 6

The combination of pineapple with sweetened condensed milk may seem a little odd at first, but this drink is most enjoyable.

....

1 pineapple, peeled, cored, and chopped
1 cup superfine sugar
3 tablespoons sweetened condensed milk
Crushed ice
Fresh mint sprigs or freshly grated nutmeg for garnish

....

In a blender, combine the pineapple, sugar, and cream or milk. Fill the container about three-fourths full with ice. Blend until smooth and slushy. Serve in your prettiest saucer Champagne glasses, garnished with mint or nutmeg.

AUNT BECKY'S JAMAICAN GINGER BEER

Makes about 4 quarts

1 whole fresh ginger root
  (4 to 6 inches long), preferably
  Jamaican ginger, peeled
  and grated
1 package (2¼ teaspoons) active
  dry yeast
4 quarts water
4 cups sugar
½ cup dark rum (optional)

Aunt Becky was a wonderful family friend who always supplied us with ginger beer from a recipe handed down through her family for many generations. Her family always used a version made with yeast, which I prefer. She also used a wonderful container called a yabba *in which to ferment her ginger beer. Yabbas are large natural clay containers glazed only on the inside. Brought to Jamaica from Africa, they are the traditional holders of everything from ginger beer to Christmas pudding and sorrel drink. While you probably have no yabbas at home, you can still enjoy making ginger beer in a large pot or jug.*

In a large stainless-steel stockpot or ceramic crock, combine the ginger, yeast, water, and sugar. Stir to blend the ingredients and dissolve the yeast. Cover and place outside in the sun for 12 hours. A temperature of 80°F is perfect for fermentation. Add the rum if you wish, or wait and add rum to each glass as you serve, for those who like a stronger drink. Strain, pour into clean glass bottles or jars with lids, and refrigerate for up to 1 week.

TAMARIND-ADE
Serves 6 to 8

15 to 20 tamarind pods
1 cup sugar, plus up to ½ cup
    to taste
6 cups warm water
About 6 cups cold water

The tamarind, a large tree with long, brown pod-type fruits, originated in India, but has been grown in Jamaica since the 1700s. A drink made from its pods is well known as a thirst quencher. When I was growing up in Jamaica, we kept a big pitcher of tamarind-ade in the refrigerator to offer to guests and visitors. It is also frequently served with ginger ale for fancy events.

Look for tamarind pods (or tamarind concentrate) in Latino and Caribbean food stores.

Remove the thin outer shell of the tamarind pods. In a large bowl, combine the pods, the 1 cup of sugar, and the warm water. Stir to dissolve the sugar and let soak for 30 to 40 minutes. Strain through a sieve into a bowl, pushing the pulp through the sieve with the back of a large spoon. Discard the seeds and solids that are left in the sieve.

Put the pulp in a large pitcher and add the cold water and the reserved sugar (2 tablespoons at a time), stirring and tasting until the combination of tart, sweet, and refreshing pleases you. You may need more than 6 cups of cold water to get the right balance! Refrigerate for at least 1 hour before serving.

SORREL DRINK
Serves 6 to 8

We always planted our sorrel in time to be ready at Christmas, although legend has it that Christmas is when the sorrel will be ready, regardless of when you plant it! At any rate, the first thing you will hear when you visit any house at Christmas is, "Have a glass of sorrel. Ours is the best you will find this year!"

2 ounces dried sorrel (available wherever Caribbean foods are sold)
1-inch piece fresh ginger, peeled and crushed
2 quarts boiling water
About 3 cups sugar (depending on how sweet you want it)
½ cup rum (optional)
Ice for serving

In a large bowl, combine the sorrel and ginger. Pour the boiling water over all, cover, and let steep for at least 24 hours. Strain through a sieve and stir in the sugar until dissolved. Add the rum, if desired. Refrigerate for at least 1 hour. Serve over ice.

SIMPLE SYRUP
Makes 1 cup

In Jamaica, we use simple syrup or grenadine syrup to sweeten our drinks. Simple syrup is easier to dissolve in cold drinks than sugar.

1 cup water
1 cup sugar

In a small saucepan, bring the water to a boil and stir in the sugar. Simmer for a few minutes, stirring until the sugar has dissolved. Let cool, cover, and refrigerate indefinitely

Resources for Jamaican and Caribbean Cooking

BOOKS

Busha Browne, *Busha Browne's Indispensable Compendium of Traditional Jamaican Cookery,* 1993.

Virginia Burke, *Eat Caribbean: The Best of Caribbean Cookery,* 2005.

Virginia Burke, *Walkerswood Caribbean Kitchen,* 2001.

John Demers, *Authentic Recipes from Jamaica,* 2005.

Enid Donaldson, *The Real Taste of Jamaica,* 2000.

Vivien Goldman, *Pearl's Delicious Jamaican Dishes,* 1992.

Dunstan Harris, *Island Barbecue; Spirited Recipes from the Caribbean,* 1995.

Jinx and Jefferson Morgan, *The Sugar Mill Caribbean Cookbook,* 1996, Harvard Common Press.

Rosemary Parkinson, *Culinaria: The Caribbean; A Culinary Discovery,* 1999.

Yvonne Sobers, *Delicious Jamaica: Vegetarian Cuisine,* 1996.

FOOD PRODUCTS

BUSHA BROWNE

Makers of Jamaican seasonings and condiments. With Walkerswood, Busha Browne products are among the most popular and widely available Jamaican food products. Order them online on their web site.
http://www.bushabrowne.com

GOYA FOODS

Producer of a variety of Caribbean and Latin American food products.
http://www.goya.com

WALKERSWOOD

Makers of Jamaican seasonings, condiments, and other foodstuffs. Walkerswood started in 1978 as a community's effort to create employment for themselves. The company's products are widely available in the Caribbean, North America, and the U.K., and can be ordered online.
http://www.walkerswood.com

INDEX